Table Of Contents

Chapter 1: Understanding Mindset Mastery

In order to truly master your mindset, it is essential to first understand what mindset is and how it influences your thoughts, beliefs, and actions. Your mindset is essentially the lens through which you see the world and interpret your experiences. It shapes your attitudes, reactions, and behaviours in response to the events and challenges you face.

There are two primary types of mindsets that people tend to have: a fixed mindset and a growth mindset. A fixed mindset is characterized by the belief that your abilities and intelligence are innate and cannot be changed. People with a fixed mindset tend to avoid challenges, give up easily, and see failures as a reflection of their abilities.

On the other hand, a growth mindset is based on the belief that your abilities can be developed through dedication and hard work. Individuals with a growth mindset embrace challenges, persist in the face of setbacks, and see failures as opportunities for learning and growth. Understanding the differences between these two mindsets is crucial for mastering your own mindset.

By recognizing your own beliefs and attitudes towards challenges and failures, you can begin to shift towards a growth mindset and unlock your full potential. Mindset mastery goes beyond just changing your attitude towards challenges; it is a holistic approach to personal development and self-improvement.

It requires developing a growth mindset not only in your professional life but also in your personal relationships, health, and overall well-being. To truly master your mindset, you must cultivate self-awareness and mindfulness to understand the patterns of thinking and behaviours that may be holding you back.

This introspection allows you to challenge your limiting beliefs and replace them with empowering beliefs that support your growth and success. Mindset mastery also involves developing resilience in the face of adversity and setbacks.

By viewing failures as opportunities for learning and growth, you can bounce back stronger and more determined to achieve your goals. Furthermore, mindset mastery encompasses the practice of positive thinking and visualization.

By envisioning your goals and dreams as already achieved, you can create a powerful psychological blueprint for success and manifest your desires into reality. This practice of mental rehearsal and positive affirmation reinforces your belief in your abilities and motivates you to take consistent action towards your goals.

Moreover, mastering your mindset requires fostering a growth-oriented environment and surrounding yourself with supportive and like-minded individuals.

By seeking out mentors, coaches, and peers who share your values and vision, you can enhance your personal development journey and accelerate your progress towards success. Ultimately, mindset mastery is a lifelong journey of self-discovery, growth, and transformation. It requires dedication, discipline, and a commitment to continuous learning and improvement.

By harnessing the power of your mindset, you can shape your reality and create the life you truly desire.

The Power of Mindset in Entrepreneurship

In the dynamic and ever-evolving world of entrepreneurship, the role of mindset cannot be underestimated. A growth mindset serves as the cornerstone of success for entrepreneurs, shaping their approach to challenges, opportunities, and overall business growth.

This mindset is grounded in a belief that intelligence, skills, and abilities can be developed through dedication, hard work, and a willingness to learn from setbacks. Cultivating a growth mindset empowers entrepreneurs to embrace uncertainty, navigate complexities, and continually push the boundaries of what is possible in their entrepreneurial journey.

Your mindset shapes how you approach challenges, setbacks, and opportunities. It determines your ability to adapt, innovate, and persevere in the face of obstacles.

Mindset Mastery for Entrepreneurs: Unlocking Your Full Potential

A key characteristic of a growth mindset is the intrinsic motivation to seek out new experiences, learn from failures, and continuously improve one's skills and strategies. This thirst for knowledge and self-improvement enables entrepreneurs to stay ahead of the curve, adapt to changing market dynamics, and innovate in their respective industries.

By viewing challenges as opportunities for growth and development, entrepreneurs with a growth mindset approach obstacles with a sense of curiosity, resilience, and determination, rather than fear or avoidance. Moreover, a growth mindset fosters a culture of innovation and creativity within entrepreneurial ventures.

Entrepreneurs who embrace this mindset are more likely to think outside the box, challenge conventional wisdom, and explore new possibilities for growth and expansion. By encouraging experimentation, risk-taking, and a willingness to pivot in response to feedback, entrepreneurs with a growth mindset create a fertile ground for disruptive ideas and game-changing innovations that can propel their businesses to new heights.

Mindset Mastery for Entrepreneurs: Unlocking Your Full Potential

Resilience is another hallmark trait of entrepreneurs with a growth mindset. Instead of being discouraged by setbacks or failures, these individuals view them as valuable learning opportunities that can inform future decisions and actions.

By reframing failure as a stepping stone to success, entrepreneurs with a growth mindset are able to bounce back quickly, learn from their mistakes, and iterate on their strategies to achieve better outcomes in the future.

In addition to resilience, a growth mindset can attract a wealth of opportunities and resources to entrepreneurs.

The positive energy, optimism, and confidence exuded by individuals with a growth mindset can inspire trust among stakeholders, attract top talent, and forge strategic partnerships that are instrumental in driving business growth and sustainability.

By radiating a can-do attitude and a spirit of continuous improvement, entrepreneurs with a growth mindset create a ripple effect that not only benefits their businesses but also their broader network and community.

In conclusion, the power of mindset in entrepreneurship is a force to be reckoned with. Entrepreneurs who cultivate a growth mindset empower themselves to embrace challenges, innovate relentlessly, and persevere in the face of adversity.

By embodying the qualities of resilience, curiosity, and a thirst for self-improvement, entrepreneurs with a growth mindset unlock their full potential and pave the way for long-term success and fulfilment in the dynamic landscape of entrepreneurship.

On the other hand, a fixed mindset can hold you back in entrepreneurship. This mindset is characterized by a belief that your abilities and intelligence are fixed traits that cannot be changed. With a fixed mindset, you may avoid challenges, give up easily, and view failures as a reflection of your abilities.

To unlock your full potential as an entrepreneur, you must cultivate a growth mindset. This means embracing challenges, learning from failures, seeking feedback, and constantly striving to improve. By developing a growth mindset, you can overcome obstacles, adapt to change, and achieve success in the competitive world of entrepreneurship.

Common Mindset Challenges for Entrepreneurs

Entrepreneurs grapple with a myriad of unique challenges when it comes to mindset that can significantly impact their ability to navigate the dynamic landscape of business ownership. The pressures they face are multifaceted, ranging from the relentless pursuit of success in a competitive marketplace to the looming specter of failure that shadows every decision.

The entrepreneur's journey is fraught with uncertainty, and the ability to cultivate a resilient mindset is crucial for weathering the inevitable storms of entrepreneurship.

At the core of many mindset challenges faced by entrepreneurs is the fear of failure. This fear can be all-consuming, stemming from the high stakes involved in running a business and the potential consequences of missteps. The fear of failure can manifest as a paralyzing force, preventing entrepreneurs from taking the risks necessary for growth and innovation.

It can lead to a mindset of playing it safe, avoiding challenges or opportunities that could potentially yield great rewards but also come with inherent risks.

Imposter syndrome is another insidious mindset challenge that plagues entrepreneurs, regardless of their level of success.

Despite external validation and accomplishments, entrepreneurs may still wrestle with feelings of inadequacy and self-doubt, often attributing their success to luck rather than their own skills and efforts. This sense of fraudulence can erode their confidence and self-esteem, making it difficult to assert themselves or make bold decisions that could propel their businesses forward.

Moreover, overwhelm and burnout are constant companions on the entrepreneurial journey. The never-ending demands of running a business, coupled with the pressure to deliver results and meet expectations, can take a toll on an entrepreneur's mental and emotional well-being.

The incessant juggling of tasks, responsibilities, and decisions can lead to a state of chronic stress that impairs judgement and clarity, making it challenging to think strategically and make sound decisions for the business. Perfectionism, while often viewed as a virtue, can also be a double-edged sword for entrepreneurs.

Mindset Mastery for Entrepreneurs: unlocking Your Full Potential

The pursuit of perfection can lead to analysis paralysis, where entrepreneurs become so consumed with getting everything right that they are unable to move forward or take decisive action. This fixation on flawlessness can hinder innovation, creativity, and adaptability, key qualities that are essential for navigating the uncertain and ever-evolving business landscape.

Furthermore, entrepreneurs frequently neglect their own well-being in the pursuit of their business goals. The glorification of hustle culture and the myth of the entrepreneurial hero often lead entrepreneurs to prioritize work over self-care, sacrificing their physical and mental health in the process.

Neglecting self-care practices such as exercise, proper nutrition, and relaxation can have serious repercussions on an entrepreneur's overall well-being, leading to burnout, decreased resilience, and a diminished capacity to lead effectively. To navigate these complex mindset challenges, entrepreneurs must proactively cultivate a growth mindset that embraces challenges, learns from failures, and embraces opportunities for growth and development.

Mindset Mastery for Entrepreneurs: Unlocking Your Full Potential

Seeking support from mentors, coaches, and peers can provide invaluable insights and perspectives, helping entrepreneurs gain clarity, confidence, and resilience in the face of adversity.

Additionally, prioritizing self-care practices such as regular exercise, mindfulness, and adequate rest can enhance mental and emotional well-being, enabling entrepreneurs to show up as their best selves and lead their businesses with clarity and purpose.

The Benefits of Developing a Growth Mindset

A growth mindset is a fundamental belief system that shapes how individuals approach challenges, setbacks, and opportunities for learning and growth. This mindset is characterized by the belief that intelligence, abilities, and talents are not fixed but can be developed and improved over time through effort, perseverance, and learning.

One of the key benefits of cultivating a growth mindset is increased resilience in the face of adversity. Individuals with a growth mindset are better equipped to navigate and bounce back from setbacks and failures. They see challenges as opportunities to learn and grow, rather than insurmountable obstacles.

This resilience allows them to persevere in the face of difficulties and continue moving forward toward their goals with a sense of optimism and determination. Developing a growth mindset also fosters a positive attitude towards learning and personal development. People with this mindset are more likely to embrace new experiences, seek feedback, and take on challenges that push them out of their comfort zone.

They understand that failure is a natural part of the learning process and view mistakes as opportunities for improvement and growth. This open-minded approach to learning enables individuals to expand their knowledge, skills, and capabilities, leading to personal and professional growth.

Furthermore, a growth mindset promotes a sense of empowerment and agency. Individuals with this mindset take ownership of their actions and choices, recognizing that they have the power to shape their own outcomes through their efforts and determination.

This sense of agency inspires self-confidence and a proactive approach to overcoming obstacles and achieving goals.

Another significant benefit of a growth mindset is increased motivation and perseverance. When individuals believe that their efforts can lead to improvement and mastery, they are more willing to invest time and energy in pursuing their goals. This intrinsic motivation propels them to persist in the face of challenges, setbacks, and obstacles, fueling a continuous cycle of learning, growth, and achievement.

In conclusion, developing a growth mindset can have a profound impact on personal growth, resilience, motivation, and success. By embracing the belief that intelligence and abilities are malleable and can be developed through effort and learning, individuals empower themselves to overcome challenges, embrace opportunities for growth, and reach their full potential.

Cultivating a growth mindset is not only a powerful tool for personal development but also a mindset shift that can lead to greater fulfilment and success in all areas of life.

Overall, developing a growth mindset is essential for entrepreneurs, professionals, business owners, and ambitious individuals who want to unlock their full potential. By embracing this mindset, you can build resilience, adapt to change, foster curiosity, and take risks that can propel you towards your goals and dreams.

So, cultivate a growth mindset and watch as your business and career thrive like never before.

Chapter 2: Identifying Limiting Beliefs

In order to truly understand and overcome limiting beliefs, it is essential to delve into the psychology behind their formation and how they impact our thought patterns and behaviours. Limiting beliefs stem from various sources, including childhood experiences, cultural conditioning, societal norms, and personal traumas.

These beliefs can be internalized over time, creating a lens through which we view ourselves and the world. Throughout our lives, we are bombarded with messages and expectations from the media, society, and those around us, shaping our beliefs about what we can achieve and who we can become.

These external influences can plant seeds of doubt and insecurity, leading us to adopt limiting beliefs about our worth, capabilities, and potential for success.

Moreover, our own experiences and setbacks can reinforce these beliefs, creating a self-perpetuating cycle of negative thinking and self-doubt. For example, a past failure or rejection may solidify the belief that we are not good enough or capable of achieving our goals, further diminishing our confidence and willingness to take risks.

The insidious nature of limiting beliefs lies in their ability to operate beneath our conscious awareness, subtly influencing our thoughts and actions without us even realizing it. These beliefs can create a sense of safety and familiarity, as stepping outside of their constraints can feel risky and uncomfortable.

To break free from the grip of limiting beliefs, it is crucial to challenge them head-on and replace them with empowering beliefs that align with our true potential and aspirations.

This process requires self-reflection, courage, and a willingness to confront the discomfort that may arise when questioning deeply ingrained beliefs about ourselves. By cultivating self-awareness and practicing self-compassion, we can begin to unravel the layers of limiting beliefs that have held us back and create space for new possibilities and growth.

Through mindful reflection, reframing negative self-talk, and seeking support from others, we can gradually shift our mindset from one of limitation to one of abundance and resilience. Ultimately, overcoming limiting beliefs is a journey of self-discovery and transformation, requiring patience, persistence, and a belief in our own capacity to rewrite the stories we tell ourselves.

By embracing our inherent worthiness and potential, we can step into our power and live a life guided by possibilities rather than limitations. As we embark on this journey of personal growth and introspection, it is important to recognize that confronting and dismantling limiting beliefs is not a linear process.

It may involve facing uncomfortable truths about ourselves, acknowledging past wounds, and challenging long-held assumptions about our capabilities. One strategy for addressing limiting beliefs is to engage in cognitive restructuring, which involves identifying and challenging negative thought patterns that reinforce self-limiting beliefs.

By examining the evidence for and against these beliefs, we can begin to replace them with more realistic and empowering perspectives. Another key aspect of overcoming limiting beliefs is building self-compassion and resilience.

By cultivating a mindset of kindness and understanding towards ourselves, we can counteract the harsh self-judgment that often accompanies limiting beliefs. Through practices such as mindfulness, meditation, and self-care, we can strengthen our inner resources and develop the resilience needed to navigate challenges and setbacks.

It is also beneficial to enlist the support of others on our journey towards overcoming limiting beliefs. Whether through therapy, mentoring, or supportive friendships, having a network of individuals who can provide encouragement, insight, and perspective can help us navigate the ups and downs of personal growth.

Ultimately, the process of overcoming limiting beliefs is an ongoing and dynamic one, requiring commitment, self-awareness, and a willingness to explore the depths of our inner world. By embracing the potential for growth and change, we can transform our relationship with ourselves and cultivate a sense of empowerment and possibility in all areas of our lives.

Recognizing Your Limiting Beliefs

In order to achieve true mindset mastery and unlock your full potential, it is essential to delve deeper into the realm of identifying and addressing your limiting beliefs. Limiting beliefs are deeply ingrained perceptions and thought patterns that act as self-imposed barriers, effectively hindering your personal growth and success in various aspects of life.

These beliefs often stem from past experiences, societal conditioning, or negative self-talk, and they can profoundly impact your mindset and behaviour. To recognize your limiting beliefs, it is important to develop a heightened sense of self-awareness and introspection.

Pay close attention to the thoughts and emotions that surface when faced with challenges or setbacks. Notice any recurring patterns of self-doubt, fear, or inadequacy that may be underlying these reactions. Journaling can be a powerful tool to track these patterns and uncover the deeply ingrained beliefs that may be holding you back. Common limiting beliefs include ideas such as "I'm not good enough," "I don't deserve happiness," or "I will never succeed."

These beliefs create a fixed mindset that reinforces a sense of powerlessness and stagnation, preventing you from taking risks and pursuing your goals with confidence. Once you have identified your limiting beliefs, the next step is to challenge and reframe them in a more empowering light.

This involves consciously shifting negative thoughts to positive affirmations and cultivating a growth mindset that embraces challenges as opportunities for growth and learning. By reframing your beliefs and internal dialogue, you can begin to dismantle the barriers that have been constraining your potential.

One powerful technique for overcoming limiting beliefs is to reframe them into positive affirmations. For example, if you believe that you are not capable of starting a successful business, reframe that belief into an affirmation such as, "I have the skills, knowledge, and determination to succeed as an entrepreneur."

It is important to remember that overcoming limiting beliefs is an ongoing process that requires dedication and self-reflection. Surrounding yourself with a supportive network, seeking guidance from mentors or professional coaches, and practicing self-care can all contribute to your journey towards mindset mastery.

By recognizing and addressing your limiting beliefs, you can create a mindset that is not only resilient in the face of challenges but also open to new possibilities and personal growth. With a mindset focused on abundance and self-empowerment, you can break free from the constraints of limiting beliefs and step into a future filled with limitless potential and fulfilment.

Further exploration of your limiting beliefs may involve exploring their origins and understanding how they have shaped your worldview and decisions up to this point. Reflect on pivotal moments in your life where these beliefs may have first taken root and consider how they have influenced your behaviour and choices over time.

Engaging in therapeutic practices such as cognitive-behavioural therapy or mindfulness techniques can also aid in unravelling the deep-seated beliefs that have held you back. Furthermore, it is crucial to address any resistance or fear that may arise as you challenge your limiting beliefs.

Fear of failure, rejection, or change often underpins these beliefs, creating a sense of discomfort or anxiety when faced with the prospect of challenging them. Embracing vulnerability and stepping outside your comfort zone can be transformative in shifting these beliefs and opening yourself up to new possibilities.

As you continue to navigate the terrain of your mindset and beliefs, remember that self-compassion and patience are key elements in this journey. Be kind to yourself as you confront and transform your limiting beliefs, recognizing that growth and change take time and effort.

Celebrate your progress and achievements along the way, acknowledging the courage it takes to confront deeply ingrained beliefs and pave the way for a more empowered and fulfilling life.

By recognizing and addressing your limiting beliefs, you can unlock your full potential as an entrepreneur. You will be able to approach challenges with confidence, take calculated risks, and pursue opportunities with a growth mindset. Ultimately, overcoming your limiting beliefs will enable you to achieve greater success and fulfilment in your entrepreneurial journey.

understanding the Impact of Limiting Beliefs on Your Business

In the world of business, one of the biggest obstacles that entrepreneurs and business owners face are limiting beliefs. These are beliefs that hold us back from reaching our full potential and achieving our goals. Understanding the impact of these limiting beliefs on your business is crucial in order to overcome them and unlock your true potential.

Limiting beliefs are often formed early in life, based on experiences, upbringing, and societal norms. These beliefs can manifest as thoughts such as "I'm not good enough," "I don't deserve success," or "I'm not smart enough to run a successful business." These beliefs can be deeply ingrained in our subconscious mind, affecting our thoughts, actions, and ultimately, our results in business.

Limiting beliefs can have a profound and pervasive impact on an individual's business success, shaping the way they perceive their capabilities, opportunities, and potential for growth. These beliefs often stem from past experiences, societal conditioning, fear of failure, or comparisons with others, creating mental barriers that inhibit progress and limit possibilities.

Within the realm of entrepreneurship, limiting beliefs can manifest in a variety of ways, hindering an individual's ability to start, expand, or sustain a successful business venture. Often, these beliefs may centre on self-perceptions of inadequacy, imposter syndrome, or an inherent fear of taking risks and stepping outside of one's comfort zone.

One common limiting belief is the notion that success is reserved for a select few and that one lacks the innate qualities or skills necessary to achieve significant accomplishments in the business world. This self-imposed barrier can lead to a lack of confidence, reluctance to pursue innovative ideas, and a constant state of self-doubt that undermines the entrepreneurial spirit.

Moreover, limiting beliefs can impact how individuals approach challenges and opportunities within their businesses, influencing decision-making processes, risk tolerance, and overall strategic direction. Those held captive by these beliefs may shy away from confronting obstacles head-on, avoiding situations where failure is a possibility, and ultimately stunting their personal and professional growth.

In interactions with others in the business landscape, limiting beliefs can also influence communication styles, networking efforts, and relationship-building strategies. Individuals harbouring beliefs of unworthiness or inferiority may struggle to assert themselves, engage in effective negotiation practices, or cultivate meaningful connections that are vital for business success.

When we operate from a place of limiting beliefs, we limit our growth potential, hinder our decision-making abilities, and sabotage our chances of success. These beliefs can lead to self-doubt, fear of failure, and a lack of confidence in our abilities. They can also prevent us from taking risks, pursuing opportunities, and achieving our goals.

To overcome limiting beliefs and unleash your full potential as an entrepreneur, it's important to first identify and acknowledge these beliefs. Take some time to reflect on your thoughts, feelings, and behaviors in relation to your business. Are there any recurring patterns or negative self-talk that may be holding you back?

To overcome these deeply ingrained limiting beliefs, individuals must embark on a journey of self-discovery, reflection, and personal growth. By challenging these negative thought patterns and replacing them with affirming, empowering beliefs, individuals can begin to reshape their mental landscape and unlock their full potential for success.

Seeking out support from mentors, business coaches, or like-minded peers can provide invaluable guidance, encouragement, and a fresh perspective on one's capabilities and potential. Surrounding oneself with a supportive network of individuals who believe in their abilities and encourage growth can foster a positive mindset and provide the necessary push to overcome limiting beliefs and seize new opportunities.

By acknowledging the profound impact of limiting beliefs on business success and taking proactive steps to counteract their influence, individuals can break free from self-imposed constraints, cultivate a mindset of abundance and possibility, and chart a path towards greater achievements in their entrepreneurial endeavours.

Breaking free from limiting beliefs requires a willingness to challenge one's own assumptions, confront fears of failure, and embrace a growth mindset that acknowledges setbacks as opportunities for learning and improvement. It involves a conscious effort to reframe negative thoughts, cultivate self-confidence, and develop resilience in the face of adversity.

Moreover, engaging in regular self-reflection and introspection can help individuals identify the root causes of their limiting beliefs and work towards dismantling them systematically.

By tracing these beliefs back to their origins and reframing them in a more positive light, individuals can gradually shift their mindset towards one of empowerment, abundance, and possibility. Additionally, incorporating practices such as visualization, affirmations, and mindfulness can help individuals reprogram their subconscious mind and instil new, empowering beliefs that align with their goals and aspirations.

By consistently reinforcing these positive beliefs through daily habits and practices, individuals can create a solid foundation for success and unlock their full potential in the entrepreneurial arena. Ultimately, breaking free from limiting beliefs is a transformative journey that requires courage, dedication, and a commitment to personal growth and development.

By recognizing the power of their thoughts and beliefs in shaping their reality, individuals can cultivate a mindset of abundance, resilience, and unwavering belief in their own capabilities, paving the way for unprecedented success and fulfillment in their entrepreneurial pursuits.

Once you've identified your limiting beliefs, challenge them by replacing them with empowering beliefs. Affirmations, visualization techniques, and mindset exercises can help reprogram your subconscious mind and shift your perspective towards a more positive and empowering mindset.

By understanding the impact of limiting beliefs on your business and taking proactive steps to overcome them, you can unlock your full potential, achieve your goals, and create the success you desire as an entrepreneur. Remember, your mindset is a powerful tool that can either propel you forward or hold you back — choose wisely.

Strategies for Overcoming Limiting Beliefs

In the world of entrepreneurship, one of the biggest obstacles that many individuals face is the presence of limiting beliefs. These are the negative thoughts and ideas that hold us back from reaching our full potential and achieving our goals. However, with the right strategies and mindset, it is possible to overcome these limiting beliefs and unlock your full potential as an entrepreneur.

One of the most effective strategies for overcoming limiting beliefs is to identify and challenge them head-on. Take the time to reflect on the beliefs that are holding you back and question their validity. Are these beliefs based on facts or are they simply assumptions that you have made about yourself or your abilities? By challenging these beliefs, you can begin to see them for what they truly are - barriers that can be overcome.

Another powerful strategy for overcoming limiting beliefs is to reframe your mindset. Instead of focusing on what you can't do or what you lack, shift your focus to what you can do and the strengths that you possess. By adopting a growth mindset and focusing on your abilities and potential, you can start to break free from the chains of limiting beliefs and open yourself up to new opportunities and possibilities.

Additionally, surrounding yourself with positive and supportive individuals can also help you overcome limiting beliefs. Seek out mentors, colleagues, and friends who believe in your potential and can offer encouragement and guidance. By building a strong support network, you can gain the confidence and motivation needed to challenge your limiting beliefs and push past your comfort zone.

Identifying and overcoming limiting beliefs is a crucial step in mindset mastery. These beliefs, often formed in our early childhood or as a result of past experiences, can create barriers to our personal and professional growth. They are deeply ingrained in our subconscious and can manifest as self-doubt, fear of failure, or a sense of unworthiness.

However, with the right strategies and mindset shifts, we can challenge and change these beliefs to create a more empowered and fulfilling life. To begin the process of overcoming limiting beliefs, it is essential to first become aware of them. This requires a level of self-reflection and introspection to identify the negative self-talk or doubts that may arise in our minds.

By recognizing and acknowledging these beliefs, we can then take steps to address them.

Taking consistent action towards our goals is also crucial in overcoming limiting beliefs. By breaking down our objectives into manageable steps and making progress each day, we can build confidence and self-assurance in our abilities. As we experience success and achievement, we reinforce the belief that we are capable of overcoming challenges and reaching our full potential.

Remember, overcoming limiting beliefs is a journey that requires commitment, self-reflection, and determination. By implementing these strategies and adopting a growth mindset, you can break free from the constraints of limiting beliefs and unlock your full potential as an entrepreneur.

Chapter 3: Cultivating a Growth Mindset

In the exploration of the growth mindset, we delve into the intricate workings of the human psyche and the profound implications this paradigm shift holds for personal development and achievement. At its essence, a growth mindset is grounded in the belief that our abilities and intelligence are not fixed but malleable, capable of expanding and evolving through deliberate effort, dedication, and resilience.

Drawing from the burgeoning field of neuroscience, we come to appreciate the remarkable phenomenon of neuroplasticity that underpins the concept of a growth mindset. The brain's capacity to rewire itself in response to new experiences and learning is a testament to the incredible adaptability and potential for growth that resides within each individual.

By immersing ourselves in challenging tasks and embracing opportunities for intellectual and emotional growth, we actively engage the brain's plasticity, fostering the development of new neural connections and pathways that enrich our cognitive abilities and broaden our horizons.

Furthermore, the cultivation of a growth mindset involves a fundamental shift in our perception of setbacks and failures. Rather than viewing these obstacles as insurmountable roadblocks, individuals with a growth mindset approach them with a sense of optimism and determination.

They see setbacks not as reflections of their innate abilities but as temporary setbacks that can be overcome through perseverance, introspection, and a willingness to learn from the experience. In doing so, they unlock the transformative power of failure, turning it into a catalyst for personal growth and self-improvement.

Central to the framework of a growth mindset is the concept of feedback and its profound impact on our learning and development. Embracing constructive criticism not as a critique of our worth but as a valuable source of information for improvement, individuals with a growth mindset actively seek out feedback and use it as a stepping stone to enhance their skills and knowledge.

By approaching feedback with an open mind and a willingness to adapt and grow, they demonstrate a profound commitment to continuous learning and self-improvement. In essence, the journey toward a growth mindset is a profound voyage of self-discovery and transformation.

By embracing the inherent potential for growth and development within ourselves, we set forth on a path of boundless possibility and endless learning. Through the conscious cultivation of a growth mindset, we unlock the door to our true potential, propelling ourselves toward new heights of excellence and fulfilment in all facets of our lives.

Embracing a Positive Attitude Towards Failure

TFailure is often viewed through a lens of disappointment and defeat, a dreaded outcome that we strive to avoid at all costs. In a society that glorifies success and achievement, the mere thought of failure can instill fear and apprehension in even the most resilient individuals. However, what if we shift our perspective and embrace failure as a crucial stepping stone on the path to growth and self-improvement?

In the world of entrepreneurship, failure is often seen as a taboo subject. Many entrepreneurs, professionals, and business owners fear failure and will go to great lengths to avoid it. However, the truth is that failure is an inevitable part of the journey to success. Instead of fearing failure, it's important to embrace a positive attitude towards it.

When faced with failure, our initial reaction may be one of frustration, self-doubt, and a sense of inadequacy. We may question our abilities, our decisions, and our worth, allowing negative thoughts to consume our minds and dampen our spirits.

Yet, buried beneath the rubble of our shattered expectations lies a hidden opportunity – an opportunity to learn, to evolve, and to emerge stronger than before. By reframing failure as a valuable learning experience, we unlock a treasure trove of insights and lessons that can shape our future endeavors. Rather than succumbing to defeat, we can harness the power of failure to propel us forward on our journey towards success.

Through introspection and analysis, we can dissect the events leading to our setback, identify the root causes of our failure, and extract invaluable nuggets of wisdom that pave the way for future victories. One of the greatest gifts of failure is the resilience and grit it instils within us. As we navigate the turbulent waters of disappointment and setback, we develop a fortitude that enables us to weather life's storms with grace and determination.

Failure becomes not a mark of shame or weakness, but a badge of honour that signifies our willingness to take risks, to push boundaries, and to dare greatly in the pursuit of our dreams. Moreover, embracing failure as a learning opportunity fosters a growth mindset that is essential for personal and professional development. By viewing setbacks as temporary roadblocks rather than insurmountable obstacles, we open ourselves up to a world of possibilities and potential.

We become more adaptable, more open to feedback, and more receptive to change, setting the stage for continuous growth and improvement in all aspects of our lives. In conclusion, failure is not the end of the road but a crossroads where new opportunities and insights await us. By embracing failure as a vital part of our growth journey, we can transform setbacks into stepping stones towards success.

Let us not fear failure, but welcome it with open arms as a teacher, a mentor, and a catalyst for personal and professional advancement. Failure serves as a mirror that reflects our vulnerabilities and weaknesses, offering us a rare glimpse into the depths of our character and resilience. It unveils the cracks in our armour, exposing areas for growth and development that we may have overlooked in the absence of setbacks.

One key aspect of embracing a positive attitude towards failure is to adopt a growth mindset. This mindset views failure as a temporary setback, rather than a reflection of our abilities or worth. With a growth mindset, we can see failure as a chance to learn, improve, and ultimately succeed.

By confronting failure head-on, we confront ourselves – our fears, insecurities, and limitations – with a level of honesty and courage that propels us towards profound self-discovery and transformation. Furthermore, failure acts as a humbling force that tempers our ego and cultivates empathy and compassion towards others who may be navigating similar challenges.

It fosters a sense of humility that reminds us of our humanity and interconnectedness with fellow travellers on the road to success. In sharing our stories of failure and resilience, we not only inspire others to persevere in the face of adversity but also create a sense of camaraderie and solidarity that binds us together in our shared quest for growth and fulfilment.

Another important aspect of embracing failure is to not dwell on the past, but instead focus on the future. Instead of letting failure hold you back, use it as motivation to push forward and strive for even greater achievements.

By seeing failure as a valuable learning opportunity and a chance for growth, you can unlock your full potential and achieve greater success in your endeavours.

Ultimately, embracing failure as a learning opportunity is not just a mindset shift but a paradigm shift that redefines our relationship with success and setbacks. It empowers us to embrace uncertainty and ambiguity with a sense of curiosity and wonder, embracing the unknown as a realm of infinite possibilities and growth.

Failure, far from being a defeat, becomes a beacon of hope and resilience that lights the way towards a future defined not by our stumbles but by our unwavering commitment to rise, learn, and evolve with each new challenge we face.

Remember, failure is not the end, but rather a stepping stone on the path to success.

Developing Resilience in the Face of Challenges

In the fast-paced world of entrepreneurship, challenges are inevitable. From financial setbacks to market competition, entrepreneurs face numerous obstacles that can test their resilience. Developing resilience is crucial for navigating these challenges and ultimately achieving success in the business world.

Just as in the business world, in our normal day to day life, we will inevitably face challenges and obstacles that test our resilience and ability to persevere. Developing resilience is a key ingredient in overcoming these challenges and emerging stronger on the other side. Resilience is not something we are born with; it is a skill that can be developed and nurtured over time.

Resilience is the ability to bounce back from setbacks, adapt to change, and persevere in the face of adversity. It is a mindset that enables entrepreneurs to stay focused, motivated, and determined, even when things don't go as planned. It is about staying strong and positive when times are tough, and finding ways to keep moving forward despite the obstacles in your path.

By cultivating resilience, entrepreneurs can overcome obstacles, learn from failures, and grow both personally and professionally. So, how can you develop resilience in the face of challenges? Here are some key strategies to help you build your resilience:

1. Embrace failure as a learning opportunity: Instead of viewing failure as a defeat, see it as a chance to learn and grow. Reflect on your mistakes, identify areas for improvement, and use your failures as stepping stones to success.

2. Stay positive and optimistic: Maintaining a positive mindset is essential for building resilience. Focus on the things you can control, practice gratitude, and surround yourself with supportive and uplifting people.

3. Take care of yourself: Physical and mental well-being are crucial for resilience. Make time for self-care, exercise regularly, get enough sleep, and practice mindfulness to reduce stress and boost your resilience.

4. Seek support: Don't be afraid to ask for help when you need it. Surround yourself with a strong support network of mentors, friends, and fellow entrepreneurs who can offer guidance, advice, and encouragement during challenging times.

One way to develop resilience is to cultivate a positive mindset. This involves reframing negative thoughts and beliefs into more positive and empowering ones. By shifting your perspective and focusing on the opportunities for growth and learning that challenges present, you can build a foundation of resilience that will help you navigate the toughest of times.

Another important aspect of resilience is self-care. Taking care of your physical, emotional, and mental well-being is essential for building resilience. This can include practices such as exercise, meditation, journaling, and seeking support from loved ones or a therapist when needed. Making self-care a priority will help you stay strong and resilient in the face of adversity.

Additionally, developing strong problem-solving skills can help you navigate challenges more effectively. By breaking down problems into manageable steps, seeking feedback and advice from others, and remaining flexible in your approach, you can build your resilience and confidence in handling difficult situations. Building resilience is also about understanding your strengths and weaknesses and recognizing that it's okay to ask for help when needed.

Seeking support from others, whether it be friends, family, colleagues, or professionals, can provide a different perspective and valuable input that can help you overcome challenges more effectively.

Furthermore, resilience is about embracing change and uncertainty. The ability to adapt to new circumstances, pivot when necessary, and remain grounded in the face of the unknown is a hallmark of resilient individuals.

By being open to change and seeing it as an opportunity for growth rather than a threat, you can strengthen your resilience and face challenges with a sense of confidence and determination.

In conclusion, developing resilience is a continuous journey that requires self-awareness, self-care, problem-solving skills, and a supportive network. By cultivating a positive mindset, practicing self-care, seeking support, and embracing change, you can build the resilience needed to thrive in the face of adversity.

Remember that resilience is not about being invincible; it's about being adaptable, proactive, and open to growth. Embrace your challenges as opportunities for learning and growth, and you will emerge stronger and more resilient than ever before.

Adopting a Learning Mindset for Continuous Improvement

In a world that is constantly evolving and changing, it is essential to adopt a learning mindset for continuous improvement. This mindset is rooted in the belief that there is always room for growth and development, and that learning is a lifelong journey.

Adopting a learning mindset is essential for entrepreneurs looking to achieve continuous improvement and unlock their full potential. In today's fast-paced and ever-changing business landscape, the ability to adapt and learn quickly is a crucial skill for success.

Embracing a learning mindset means being open to new ideas, feedback, and experiences. It requires a willingness to challenge your existing beliefs and assumptions, and to be open to new perspectives. By approaching life with a learning mindset, you can continually expand your knowledge, skills, and understanding of the world around you.

One key aspect of adopting a learning mindset is embracing failure as a natural part of the learning process. Instead of viewing failure as a setback, see it as an opportunity to learn and grow. By reframing failure in this way, you can overcome fear and perfectionism, and instead, focus on experimentation and continuous improvement.

Moreover, cultivating a learning mindset involves seeking out new challenges and opportunities to expand your skills and knowledge. Whether it's taking on a new project at work, learning a new hobby, or enrolling in a course, embracing new challenges can help you push past your comfort zone and develop new capabilities. In essence, adopting a learning mindset is about recognizing that growth and improvement are ongoing processes.

By staying curious, open-minded, and willing to learn, you can unlock your full potential and achieve continuous personal and professional growth. Furthermore, developing a learning mindset also involves cultivating a growth-oriented attitude towards setbacks and obstacles. Instead of viewing challenges as insurmountable barriers, those with a learning mindset see them as opportunities for growth and development.

They approach difficulties with resilience, seeking to learn from their experiences and emerge stronger and more capable as a result.

Additionally, building a supportive network of mentors, peers, and colleagues can be instrumental in fostering a learning mindset. Surrounding yourself with individuals who inspire, challenge, and support your growth can provide valuable insights, feedback, and encouragement as you navigate your learning journey.

Another important component of a learning mindset is the willingness to seek out feedback from others. Constructive criticism can provide valuable insights and help entrepreneurs identify areas for improvement. By actively seeking feedback and being open to suggestions, entrepreneurs can accelerate their personal and professional growth.

Collaboration and shared learning experiences can further deepen your understanding and broaden your perspective on various subjects and issues. Lastly, self-reflection and introspection play a crucial role in cultivating a learning mindset. Taking the time to reflect on your experiences, successes, and failures can provide valuable insights into your strengths, weaknesses, and areas for growth.

Through introspection, you can identify areas where you can further develop your skills and knowledge, setting goals for continuous learning and improvement. In conclusion, embracing a learning mindset is not just about acquiring new facts or skills; it is a holistic approach to personal and professional development.

By nurturing a curiosity for learning, embracing challenges, seeking out diverse perspectives, and reflecting on your journey, you can continuously evolve and thrive in an ever-changing world.

Continuous learning is also essential for staying ahead in today's competitive business environment. By staying curious and constantly seeking out new knowledge and skills, entrepreneurs can adapt to changing trends and technologies, positioning themselves as industry leaders.

In conclusion, adopting a learning mindset is key to unlocking your full potential as an entrepreneur. By embracing failure as a learning opportunity, seeking out feedback, and committing to continuous learning, you can achieve greater success and drive innovation in your business.

So, make a commitment to lifelong learning and watch your business thrive.

Chapter 4: Building Confidence and Self-Esteem

Confidence and self-esteem are fundamental aspects of our inner world that profoundly impact how we engage with the world around us. They are the bedrock upon which we stand, influencing our decisions, relationships, and overall well-being. Understanding and nurturing these qualities is a vital key to unlocking our full potential and living a fulfilling life.

Developing a deeper sense of self-awareness is where the journey to building confidence and self-esteem truly begins. This entails diving into the depths of our being to unearth our authentic selves - our values, beliefs, strengths, and weaknesses. Through introspection and reflection, we can unravel the threads of self-doubt and negative self-perception that may have woven themselves into our psyche.

By shedding light on these internal barriers, we empower ourselves to challenge and reframe them, replacing self-limiting beliefs with empowering truths that affirm our worth and capabilities. Setting meaningful and achievable goals is a cornerstone of building confidence and self-esteem. By breaking down our aspirations into actionable steps, we create a roadmap that guides us towards our vision of success.

Each milestone achieved serves as a testament to our abilities and resilience, nurturing a sense of accomplishment that fuels our confidence to take on bigger challenges and tackle obstacles with unwavering resolve. The power of our social environment cannot be understated when it comes to shaping our confidence and self-esteem. Surrounding ourselves with supportive, positive individuals who believe in our potential can be a potent source of encouragement and validation.

Seeking out mentors or role models who embody the qualities we aspire to can provide invaluable guidance and inspiration, guiding us towards greater self-awareness and growth. Self-care is a crucial element in the cultivation of confidence and self-esteem.

Nurturing our physical, emotional, and mental well-being is a form of self-respect that sends a powerful message to our inner selves. Engaging in activities that bring us joy, practicing mindfulness, and setting boundaries that honor our needs are all acts of self-love that contribute to a resilient sense of self-worth.

Building confidence and self-esteem is not a one-time feat but a lifelong journey of self-discovery and growth. Embracing setbacks as opportunities for learning and resilience, and maintaining a mindset of perseverance and self-belief, are essential components of this ongoing evolution.

By committing to our personal development and trusting in our innate potential, we can cultivate a deep reservoir of unshakeable confidence and self-worth that illuminates our path towards a life of fulfilment and purpose.

Understanding the Connection Between Confidence and Success

Confidence is a multifaceted attribute that transcends mere self-assurance and plays a pivotal role in shaping our successes and failures. It operates as a dynamic force that influences our thoughts, emotions, and behaviours, steering our actions towards achievement or stagnation. The intricate interplay between confidence and success is a complex dance of internal beliefs, external validation, and resilience in the face of adversity.

At its core, confidence is grounded in self-awareness and self-acceptance, allowing individuals to embrace their strengths, acknowledge their weaknesses, and strive for continuous improvement. This self-awareness serves as a compass, guiding individuals towards setting realistic goals, taking calculated risks, and challenging themselves to break free from comfort zones.

By cultivating a growth mindset rooted in self-compassion and determination, individuals can harness the power of confidence to propel them towards their aspirations. Moreover, the impact of confidence extends beyond personal growth and permeates our interactions with the world around us.

Confident individuals exude a magnetic aura that attracts opportunities, nurtures relationships, and fosters collaboration. Their ability to communicate effectively, assert boundaries, and navigate challenges with poise often sets them apart in various spheres of life, from professional endeavours to personal relationships.

Furthermore, the link between confidence and success is reinforced by the role of external validation in shaping our self-perception. Positive feedback from peers, mentors, and loved ones can bolster our confidence, affirm our worth, and fuel our motivation to strive for excellence.

However, true confidence transcends external approval and remains steadfast, anchored in an unwavering belief in one's abilities and potential. In essence, the journey towards success is a testament to the transformative power of confidence, a dynamic force that enables individuals to navigate life's complexities with grace, resilience, and authenticity.

By embracing self-awareness, cultivating self-compassion, and fostering a growth mindset, individuals can unlock the true potential within themselves and embark on a path of fulfillment, contribution, and meaningful success.

Confidence is not just a feeling; it is a mindset that can be cultivated and strengthened over time. By developing a positive self-image, setting achievable goals, and celebrating your successes, you can boost your confidence and increase your chances of success.

Confidence also plays a key role in how others perceive you and your business. When you exude confidence, you are more likely to attract clients, investors, and partners who believe in your vision and abilities.

Success, on the other hand, is the result of hard work, determination, and resilience. It is not always easy to achieve success, but having confidence in yourself can give you the motivation and drive to keep pushing forward, even in the face of obstacles.

By understanding the connection between confidence and success, you can harness the power of your mindset to propel your business to new heights.

Techniques for Boosting Self-Confidence

In the competitive business world, self-confidence is a crucial trait that can make or break your success. Having a strong sense of self-belief can help you overcome challenges, take risks, and seize opportunities with conviction. However, building and maintaining self-confidence is not always easy, especially in the face of setbacks and failures. That's why it's important to develop techniques that can help you boost your self-confidence and unlock your full potential as an entrepreneur.

One of the most effective techniques for boosting self-confidence is positive self-talk. The way you talk to yourself can have a powerful impact on your self-perception and overall mindset. Instead of focusing on your weaknesses and failures, try to cultivate a positive inner dialogue that reinforces your strengths and successes. Remind yourself of past accomplishments, affirm your abilities, and visualize your future success to build a strong foundation of self-confidence.

Another powerful technique for boosting self-confidence is setting and achieving small goals. By breaking down your larger aspirations into smaller, manageable tasks, you can build a sense of accomplishment and momentum that fuels your self-confidence. Celebrate your victories, no matter how small, and use them as stepping stones to propel you towards bigger goals.

Additionally, surrounding yourself with positive and supportive individuals can also boost your self-confidence. Seek out mentors, peers, or friends who believe in your abilities and can provide encouragement and guidance along your entrepreneurial journey. Their validation and support can reinforce your self-belief and help you navigate challenges with confidence.

Self-confidence is a multifaceted characteristic that influences every aspect of our lives, from our relationships to our professional endeavours. It is the foundation upon which we build our self-worth, resilience, and ability to achieve our aspirations.

Developing self-confidence requires a conscious effort and a commitment to personal growth. Here are some additional techniques to further enhance your self-confidence:

1. Embrace Failure as a Learning Opportunity: Instead of viewing failure as a reflection of your abilities, see it as a valuable lesson that can help you improve and grow. Each setback is a stepping stone toward success, and approaching failures with a growth mindset can boost your resilience and self-assurance. Embracing failure also teaches you the importance of perseverance and grit in the face of challenges.

2. Practice Mindfulness: Mindfulness encourages you to focus on the present moment without judgment. By staying present and attuned to your thoughts and feelings, you can cultivate a deeper understanding of yourself and your inner workings. This self-awareness can lead to a greater sense of self-acceptance and confidence. Mindfulness also helps reduce stress and anxiety, allowing you to approach situations with clarity and composure.

3. Seek Feedback and Constructive Criticism: Embrace feedback as a tool for self-improvement rather than criticism. Solicit constructive feedback from mentors, peers, or loved ones to gain insights into areas where you can enhance your skills and abilities. Accepting feedback gracefully demonstrates your openness to growth and can bolster your self-assurance. Actively seeking feedback shows your commitment to personal development and continuous improvement.

4. Develop a Growth Mindset: Cultivate a belief that your abilities and intelligence can be developed through effort and perseverance. Embrace challenges as opportunities to learn and grow, rather than viewing them as threats to your self-worth. A growth mindset fosters resilience, determination, and a sense of agency over your own success. It also encourages a positive attitude towards learning and adapting to new situations.

5. Engage in Self-Care Practices: Prioritize activities that nourish your mind, body, and spirit. Engaging in self-care rituals such as exercise, meditation, hobbies, or spending time in nature can replenish your energy and enhance your overall well-being. Taking care of yourself holistically can boost your self-confidence and sense of self-worth. Self-care is essential for maintaining balance and inner harmony, which are crucial for cultivating self-confidence.

6. Reflect on Your Values and Beliefs: Take time to explore your core values, beliefs, and passions. Understanding what matters most to you can provide a sense of purpose and direction in your life, bolstering your self-confidence and guiding your decision-making. Aligning your actions with your values can cultivate a sense of authenticity and confidence in yourself. Reflecting on your values also helps you stay true to yourself and maintain a strong sense of identity in the face of external pressures.

Remember, self-confidence is not a fixed trait — it's a skill that can be developed and strengthened over time with practice and dedication and a journey of self-discovery and personal growth, and each step you take toward cultivating your confidence is a testament to your inner strength and potential for greatness.

Building a Support Network for Encouragement and Feedback

In the pursuit of personal growth and self-mastery, the cultivation of a robust support network serves as a cornerstone for navigating the complexities of our journeys. These networks are more than just a collection of individuals who offer encouragement; they are intricately woven tapestries of diverse perspectives, experiences, and insights that enrich our lives in countless ways.

At the core of any strong support network are individuals who believe in our potential, even when we may doubt ourselves, and who offer unwavering support through the highs and lows of our endeavours. Friends who lift us up with their positivity, family members who provide a sense of grounding and security, mentors who share their wisdom and guidance, coaches who challenge us to push beyond our self-imposed limits, and colleagues who share in our triumphs and setbacks all play vital roles in shaping our growth and development.

Mindset Mastery for Entrepreneurs: Unlocking Your Full Potential

The beauty of a support network lies in its capacity to illuminate our blind spots and expand our horizons. When we open ourselves up to feedback and constructive criticism from those we trust, we invite opportunities for reflection, learning, and growth. Their perspectives serve as mirrors that reflect our strengths and weaknesses, helping us to see ourselves more clearly and empowering us to make meaningful changes that propel us forward.

Networking events, industry conferences, and online communities are all great places to connect with potential members of your support network. By actively seeking out these connections and nurturing relationships with individuals who share your goals and values, you can create a strong foundation of support that will help you stay focused and motivated as you work towards achieving your entrepreneurial dreams.

Sharing our dreams and aspirations within our support network not only garners encouragement but also invites collaboration and co-creation. The collective wisdom and diverse viewpoints of our network can spark new ideas, challenge our assumptions, and inspire innovative approaches that we may not have considered on our own.

Together, we can brainstorm, problem-solve, and strategize, drawing upon the collective energy and creativity of the group to overcome obstacles and reach new heights of achievement. In reciprocating the support and encouragement we receive, we contribute to a culture of empowerment and growth that benefits everyone involved.

By being a source of inspiration, motivation, and feedback for our peers, we foster an environment of trust, respect, and collaboration that amplifies the impact of our collective efforts. Together, we create a ripple effect of positive change, lifting each other up and propelling one another towards success and fulfillment. Within the rich tapestry of a supportive community, we find the strength, resilience, and inspiration needed to confront challenges, embrace opportunities, and evolve into our fullest potential.

The bonds we forge within our network serve as pillars of support, grounding us in times of uncertainty and elevating us to new heights of achievement. Together, we embark on a shared journey of growth and transformation, united by our common goal of mastering our mindset and realizing our dreams.

In addition to providing encouragement and feedback, your support network can also serve as a source of inspiration and accountability. Surrounding yourself with ambitious and motivated individuals can help fuel your own drive for success and push you to set and achieve ambitious goals. By regularly connecting with your support network, you can stay on track, overcome obstacles, and continue to grow and evolve as an entrepreneur.

In conclusion, building a support network for encouragement and feedback is essential for unlocking your full potential as an entrepreneur. By surrounding yourself with like-minded individuals who understand the challenges and rewards of entrepreneurship, you can stay motivated, inspired, and accountable as you work towards achieving your goals.

So don't be afraid to reach out, make connections, and build a strong support network that will help you succeed in your entrepreneurial journey.

Chapter 5: Setting Clear Goals and Taking Action

Setting clear goals is a fundamental aspect of achieving success in any aspect of life. Goals provide us with a sense of direction, motivation, and purpose, guiding our actions and decisions towards a specific outcome. Without clear goals, we may find ourselves wandering aimlessly, unsure of where we are heading or what we are striving to accomplish. When setting goals, it is crucial to be specific and meaningful.

Vague or generic goals do not provide the necessary clarity and focus required to make progress. Instead, defining clear, specific goals helps us understand exactly what we want to achieve and allows us to create actionable steps to reach our desired outcome. Furthermore, it is essential to set goals that are realistic and achievable. While it is important to challenge ourselves and strive for greatness, setting unattainable goals can lead to frustration and disappointment.

By setting realistic goals that stretch our capabilities but are within our reach, we increase our motivation and confidence in our ability to succeed. In addition to setting realistic goals, it is beneficial to establish a timeline for achieving them. Deadlines create a sense of urgency and accountability, pushing us to take action and make progress towards our goals.

Breaking down long-term goals into smaller, manageable tasks with associated deadlines can help us stay on track and make steady progress over time. Taking action is the key to turning our goals into reality. It is not enough to simply set goals and hope for the best — we must actively work towards achieving them. Consistent effort, dedication, and perseverance are essential qualities that help us overcome obstacles and setbacks on our journey to success.

Developing a growth mindset is also crucial when it comes to taking action on our goals. Embracing challenges, learning from failures, and seeking opportunities for growth and improvement are all part of the process of achieving our goals. By cultivating a mindset focused on progress and development, we can adapt to changing circumstances and find creative solutions to achieve our goals.

Ultimately, setting clear goals and taking consistent action towards achieving them are integral components of success. By defining specific, realistic goals, establishing a timeline, and cultivating a growth mindset, we can create a roadmap towards realizing our dreams and aspirations.

Remember, action is the bridge between our goals and our accomplishments – it is up to us to take that step and make our goals a reality.

The Importance of Goal Setting for Entrepreneurs

Setting clear goals is essential for entrepreneurs looking to achieve success in their ventures. Goals provide direction, motivation, and a roadmap for success. They help entrepreneurs focus their efforts, make better decisions, and stay on track towards their desired outcomes. When setting goals, it is crucial for entrepreneurs to be specific, measurable, achievable, relevant, and time-bound (SMART).

By adhering to the SMART criteria, entrepreneurs can ensure that their goals are realistic and attainable. This approach helps in breaking down larger objectives into smaller, manageable tasks, making the path to success more clear and achievable. Furthermore, setting specific goals enables entrepreneurs to align their actions with their vision and values. When entrepreneurs have a clear understanding of what they want to achieve and why it matters to them, they can stay motivated and committed to their goals, even in the face of challenges and setbacks.

In addition to being specific, goals should also be measurable. Establishing measurable targets allows entrepreneurs to track their progress, evaluate their performance, and make data-driven decisions. By quantifying their goals, entrepreneurs can easily determine whether they are on the right track or need to adjust their strategies to stay on course. Moreover, goals must be achievable to be effective.

While it is essential to set ambitious goals that push boundaries and drive growth, entrepreneurs must also ensure that their goals are within reach. Setting unattainable goals can lead to frustration and demotivation, ultimately hindering progress and success.

Relevance is another critical factor in goal setting. Entrepreneurs must ensure that their goals are aligned with their overall business objectives and contribute to their long-term success. Setting goals that are meaningful and relevant to the business's mission and values will increase motivation and focus, driving entrepreneurs towards sustainable growth and prosperity. Lastly, goals should be time-bound to provide a sense of urgency and accountability.

By setting deadlines and milestones, entrepreneurs can create a sense of momentum and push themselves to take consistent action towards their goals. Time-bound goals also help entrepreneurs prioritize tasks, manage their time effectively, and make steady progress towards their desired outcomes.

In conclusion, goal setting is an essential tool for entrepreneurs looking to unlock their full potential and achieve success in their ventures. Setting SMART goals that are specific, measurable, achievable, relevant, and time-bound is crucial for entrepreneurial success.

By aligning goals with their vision, tracking progress, staying adaptable, and maintaining focus and motivation, entrepreneurs can overcome challenges, seize opportunities, and stay on track to reach their objectives and achieve their business aspirations.

Whether you are a seasoned business owner or a startup entrepreneur, mastering the art of goal setting is key to realizing your dreams and building a thriving business.

Creating SMART Goals for Your Business

Creating SMART Goals for Your Business: Setting specific, measurable, achievable, relevant, and time-bound (SMART) goals is essential for the success and growth of any business. When you have well-defined objectives in place, you provide a roadmap for your team to follow and ensure that everyone is working towards a common purpose.

Let's explore each component of SMART goals in more depth to understand how you can effectively apply them to your business strategy:

1. Specific: The specific aspect of SMART goals emphasizes the importance of clearly defining what you want to achieve. When setting specific goals, consider answering the five "W" questions - who, what, where, when, and why. By providing precise details and outlining the desired outcome, you eliminate ambiguity and ensure that everyone understands the purpose of the goal. Specific goals serve as a guiding light for your team, allowing them to focus their efforts on tasks that directly contribute to achieving the overall objective.

2. Measurable: Measurable goals involve quantifiable metrics that allow you to track progress and evaluate success. By establishing measurable indicators and Key Performance Indicators (KPIs) for your goals, you can monitor performance, identify areas for improvement, and make data-driven decisions to optimize your business operations. Measuring success provides you with valuable insights into the effectiveness of your strategies and enables you to make informed adjustments to ensure you are on track to achieve your objectives.

3. Achievable: The achievable component of SMART goals emphasizes the importance of setting realistic and attainable targets for your business. While it is essential to aim high and challenge your team, setting goals that are within reach motivates and empowers your employees to strive for success. Consider factors such as resources, capabilities, and timelines when determining the achievability of your goals. By setting achievable objectives, you instil a sense of confidence in your team and foster a culture of accomplishment within your organization.

4. Relevant: The relevance of SMART goals underscores the importance of aligning your objectives with the overarching vision and priorities of your business. Ensure that your goals are directly linked to your company's strategic initiatives and contribute to its long-term success. By setting relevant goals, you enable your team to focus on activities that drive meaningful outcomes and propel your business towards its desired future state. Relevance ensures that your efforts are purposeful and strategic, leading to impactful results and sustained growth.

5. Time-bound: Time-bound goals have a defined timeframe within which they should be achieved. Establishing deadlines creates a sense of urgency and ensures that your team remains focused and driven towards meeting the goal. Setting specific timelines helps prioritize tasks, allocate resources efficiently, and track progress effectively. By implementing time-bound goals, you cultivate a culture of accountability and commitment within your team, fostering a results-driven mindset that propels your business towards success within designated timeframes.

So, in short, to summarize SMART:

Specific goals are clear and well-defined. Instead of setting a goal to "increase sales," a specific goal would be to "increase sales by 20% in the next quarter."

Measurable goals allow you to track your progress and determine if you are on track to achieve them. For example, you could measure your progress towards increasing sales by tracking monthly revenue numbers.

Achievable goals are realistic and attainable. While it's great to aim high, setting goals that are too far out of reach can be discouraging. Make sure your goals are challenging but within reach with the right effort and resources.

Relevant goals are aligned with your overall business objectives and priorities. They should contribute to the growth and success of your business.

Finally, **Time-bound goals** have a deadline or timeframe attached to them. Without a deadline, goals can drag on indefinitely, losing their sense of urgency. Setting a deadline will help you stay focused and motivated to achieve your goals in a timely manner.

Incorporating the SMART criteria into your goal-setting process equips you with a structured framework to plan, execute, and measure the effectiveness of your business objectives.

By combining specificity, measurability, achievability, relevance, and time-bound parameters, you create a strategic roadmap that guides your team towards achieving sustainable growth and success in a competitive business landscape. Regularly review and assess your goals to ensure they remain aligned with your business's evolving needs and market dynamics, making necessary adjustments to stay agile and responsive to changing circumstances.

Remember, SMART goals are not just about setting targets but also about fostering a culture of continuous improvement and innovation within your organization.

Remember to regularly review and adjust your goals as needed to ensure they remain relevant and achievable. With the right mindset and approach, you can unlock your full potential as an entrepreneur and take your business to new heights.

Strategies for Taking Consistent Action Towards Your Goals

In order to achieve success as an entrepreneur, it is crucial to take consistent action towards your goals. Without consistent action, your dreams and aspirations will remain just that – dreams. Here are some key strategies that will help you stay motivated and focused on your goals.

1. Set Clear and Specific Goals: The first step towards taking consistent action is to set clear and specific goals. Make sure your goals are realistic, measurable, and achievable. This will give you a roadmap to follow and keep you on track towards your ultimate vision.

2. Break Down Your Goals: Once you have set your goals, break them down into smaller, more manageable tasks. This will make your goals seem less overwhelming and allow you to make progress on a daily basis.

3. Create a Routine: Establishing a routine is essential for taking consistent action. Set aside dedicated time each day to work towards your goals. This will help you develop discipline and make progress even on days when you don't feel motivated.

4. Stay Accountable: Find an accountability partner who can help keep you on track. Share your goals with them and check in regularly to update them on your progress. Knowing that someone else is holding you accountable can be a powerful motivator.

5. Celebrate Your Wins: Finally, don't forget to celebrate your wins, no matter how small they may seem. Acknowledging your progress will help boost your confidence and keep you motivated to continue taking action towards your goals.

By implementing these strategies, you will be well on your way to achieving success as an entrepreneur. Remember, consistency is key, and by taking small steps each day, you will eventually reach your ultimate goals.

Chapter 6: Overcoming Procrastination and Fear

As an entrepreneur you will, undoubtedly, encounter a fair share of challenges when it comes to overcoming procrastination and fear in your growth process. These two formidable foes have the power to derail even the most seasoned entrepreneurs, but by understanding their underlying causes and implementing effective strategies, you'll learn how to navigate through them and continue producing meaningful work.

Procrastination, often fuelled by a fear of failure or a desire for perfection, can be a entrepreneur's worst enemy. It's all too easy to succumb to the temptation of putting off tasks until later, rationalizing that inspiration will strike tomorrow or that the timing isn't quite right. However, what begins as a harmless delay can quickly snowball into a significant setback, leaving you feeling overwhelmed and demotivated.

Breaking down daunting tasks into smaller, more manageable steps can be a game-changer for combating procrastination. By setting specific, achievable goals and establishing a structured timeline for completing each task, you can make steady progress without feeling overwhelmed. This approach not only helps overcoming the inertia of procrastination but also boosts your confidence as you see tangible results from your efforts.

Fear, whether it's a fear of rejection, criticism, or simply not measuring up to one's own expectations, can paralyze even the most talented individual. The nagging voice of self-doubt can chip away at your confidence and make it challenging to put your thoughts and ideas out into the world.

However, you'll come to realize that fear is a natural part of the creative and entrepreneurial process and that embracing it can lead to growth and self-discovery. Reframing your mindset is key in conquering your fears. Instead of viewing challenges as insurmountable obstacles, see them as opportunities for personal and artistic development.

By shifting your perspective and viewing setbacks as learning experiences, you will be able to cultivate resilience and tenacity in the face of adversity. Embracing discomfort and pushing yourself outside of your comfort zone will be instrumental in honing your craft and pushing the boundaries of your creativity and growth.

In conclusion, in the face of procrastination and fear, you must learn that obstacles are not insurmountable roadblocks but rather opportunities for growth and self-improvement. By breaking tasks into manageable steps, reframing your mindset, and embracing the inherent challenges of the entrepreneurial process, you will continue to evolve and thrive in your journey.

By confronting procrastination and fear head-on, you will unlock your full potential and discover the boundless possibilities that lie beyond your comfort zone.

Identifying the Root Causes of Procrastination

Procrastination is a complex behavioural issue that plagues individuals from all walks of life. It is a phenomenon that transcends age, gender, and occupation, affecting students struggling to complete assignments, professionals avoiding important tasks at work, and even creatives putting off their artistic endeavours.

The underlying reasons for procrastination are multifaceted and often deeply rooted in psychological and emotional factors. Fear of failure is one of the most common reasons why people procrastinate. The fear of not meeting expectations, of making mistakes, or of facing criticism can be paralyzing, leading individuals to delay starting or completing tasks. This fear stems from a deep-seated desire for perfection and a need for validation from others.

The idea of falling short of expectations can be so daunting that individuals would rather put off a task indefinitely than risk failure. Perfectionism, while often seen as a positive trait, can actually contribute significantly to procrastination. Those who hold themselves to impossibly high standards may delay taking action because they fear that they will not be able to meet their own lofty expectations.

The pursuit of perfection can create a sense of overwhelm and self-doubt, making it difficult to even begin a task, let alone complete it. Lack of motivation or interest in a task can also be a driving force behind procrastination. When individuals do not see the value or purpose in what they are doing, they may struggle to find the internal drive to start or finish the task.

This lack of intrinsic motivation can lead to feelings of apathy and disengagement, making it easy to put off responsibilities in favor of more immediately rewarding activities.

Furthermore, poor time management skills can exacerbate the tendency to procrastinate. Individuals who struggle to plan, prioritize, and organize their tasks effectively may find themselves constantly playing catch-up, scrambling to complete tasks at the last minute. This reliance on deadline pressure can create a cycle of procrastination, as the adrenaline rush of a looming deadline becomes a habitual source of motivation.

In order to overcome procrastination, individuals must first recognize and acknowledge the underlying reasons behind their behaviour. By addressing fears of failure, perfectionistic tendencies, motivational barriers, and time management issues, individuals can begin to develop strategies to break free from the cycle of procrastination.

This may involve setting realistic goals, breaking tasks down into smaller, manageable steps, seeking support from others, and cultivating a mindset of self-compassion and resilience. By digging deeper into the roots of procrastination, individuals can take meaningful steps towards reclaiming their time, productivity, and overall well-being.

Moreover, research has shown that procrastination is often linked to underlying psychological issues such as low self-esteem, anxiety, and depression. Individuals who struggle with perfectionism and fear of failure may be grappling with deep-seated insecurities and self-doubt that manifest as procrastination.

Therapy and counselling can be valuable tools in addressing these underlying emotional challenges, providing individuals with a safe space to explore their thoughts and feelings and develop healthier coping strategies.

Furthermore, the role of cognitive dissonance in procrastination cannot be overlooked. Cognitive dissonance theory posits that individuals experience mental discomfort when their beliefs or attitudes conflict with their actions.

In the context of procrastination, individuals may hold positive beliefs about themselves as capable and competent individuals, yet their procrastination behaviour contradicts these beliefs.

This internal conflict can lead to feelings of guilt, shame, and cognitive dissonance, perpetuating the cycle of procrastination as individuals struggle to reconcile their self-concept with their behavior. Additionally, procrastination has been linked to poor emotional regulation and impulsivity.

Individuals who have difficulty managing their emotions or delaying gratification may be more prone to putting off tasks in favour of immediate rewards or distractions.

This impulsivity can hijack the decision-making process, leading individuals to prioritize short-term pleasure over long-term goals and responsibilities. Developing emotional intelligence and impulse control skills can help individuals better regulate their emotions and impulses, reducing the urge to procrastinate and increasing their capacity for self-discipline.

In conclusion, procrastination is a multifaceted phenomenon rooted in psychological, emotional, and behavioural factors. By understanding the underlying reasons for procrastination, individuals can begin to unravel the complexities of their procrastination behaviour and take proactive steps towards overcoming this pervasive issue.

Through self-awareness, self-compassion, and strategic interventions, individuals can break free from the cycle of procrastination and cultivate a more productive and fulfilling life.

Techniques for Overcoming Fear and Taking Risks

Fear and risk-taking are inevitable parts of the entrepreneurial journey. As an entrepreneur, you will constantly be faced with decisions that require you to step outside of your comfort zone and take a leap of faith. However, fear can often hold us back from achieving our full potential and taking the necessary risks to grow our businesses.

Fear is a complex emotion that can manifest in various forms and hinder our ability to take bold, decisive actions. By delving deeper into the nuanced aspects of fear and risk-taking, we can equip ourselves with the tools and insights needed to navigate challenges and seize opportunities with confidence and clarity.

One advanced technique for conquering fear is developing emotional resilience. Emotional resilience involves building the capacity to bounce back from setbacks, adapt to change, and thrive in the face of adversity. By cultivating a mindset that embraces uncertainty and views challenges as opportunities for growth, you can enhance your ability to confront fear head-on and emerge stronger on the other side.

Practices such as journaling, self-reflection, and seeking support from mentors or mental health professionals can help you build emotional resilience and fortitude in times of uncertainty. Additionally, exploring the concept of fear setting can provide a powerful framework for dissecting and managing your fears effectively. Coined by author and speaker Tim Ferriss, fear setting involves defining your fears, outlining the worst-case scenarios, and identifying potential solutions and benefits of taking action.

By breaking down your fears into manageable components and rationalizing your concerns, you can gain clarity and perspective on the risks involved and make informed decisions that align with your values and aspirations. Another advanced strategy for overcoming fear is to leverage the power of neuroplasticity and cognitive reframing.

Neuroplasticity refers to the brain's ability to rewire and adapt to new experiences and challenges, shaping our thought patterns and emotional responses. By engaging in cognitive reframing techniques such as positive self-talk, visualization, and affirmations, you can reprogram your brain to perceive fear as a signal for growth and transformation rather than a threat to be avoided.

This shift in perspective can empower you to embrace uncertainty, take calculated risks, and pursue your goals with conviction and optimism. Furthermore, incorporating mindfulness-based practices such as yoga, meditation, or breathwork into your daily routine can enhance your ability to manage fear and anxiety effectively.

Mindfulness cultivates present-moment awareness, allowing you to observe your thoughts and emotions without judgment and respond to challenging situations with greater clarity and stability. By cultivating a mindfulness practice, you can develop inner resilience, emotional intelligence, and a sense of inner peace that supports you in facing fear and uncertainty with grace and composure.

In conclusion, mastering the art of overcoming fear and embracing risk-taking requires a multidimensional approach that combines emotional resilience, cognitive reframing, fear setting, and mindfulness practices. By integrating these advanced techniques into your daily life, you can empower yourself to step outside your comfort zone, pursue your dreams with courage and conviction, and navigate the complexities of fear and uncertainty with grace and resilience.

Developing a Productive Routine to Combat Procrastination

In today's fast-paced world, it's easy to get overwhelmed by the constant demands of work, family, and other responsibilities. Procrastination can creep in when we feel like we have too much on our plate or when we're unsure of how to tackle a task. However, developing a productive routine can help combat procrastination and allow us to make significant progress towards our goals.

One key component of combating procrastination is to create a structured routine that includes dedicated time for work, breaks, self-care, and relaxation. By establishing a schedule and sticking to it, we can train our minds to focus on the task at hand and avoid distractions. Research has shown that our brains respond well to routines and patterns.

When we consistently engage in productive habits, such as setting aside specific work hours each day and taking regular breaks to recharge, our brains become primed for focused and efficient work. This consistency helps reduce the likelihood of succumbing to procrastination and enhances our overall productivity. Breaking down tasks into smaller, manageable steps is another effective strategy for overcoming procrastination.

The sheer magnitude of a daunting task can often discourage us from starting, but by breaking it down into smaller, actionable items, we can make progress more easily. This approach not only makes the task feel more achievable but also provides a sense of accomplishment with each step completed, fuelling our motivation to continue. Setting specific goals and deadlines for each step of a task is crucial in holding ourselves accountable and maintaining momentum.

By establishing clear expectations for what needs to be done and when, we create a sense of urgency that can propel us forward and prevent procrastination from taking hold. Identifying and eliminating distractions is also key to reducing procrastination. In today's digital age, we are constantly bombarded with notifications, emails, and other interruptions that can derail our focus.

By taking proactive measures to minimize distractions, such as turning off notifications, setting boundaries with others, or using productivity tools to block tempting websites, we can create an environment conducive to deep work and concentration. In addition to structuring our workday and minimizing distractions, prioritizing self-care and well-being is essential for sustaining productivity and combating procrastination in the long term.

Engaging in regular exercise, maintaining a balanced diet, staying hydrated, and getting adequate sleep are all fundamental components of a healthy lifestyle that can enhance our cognitive function, mood, and overall well-being, making us better equipped to tackle tasks efficiently. Practicing self-compassion and forgiveness when we do succumb to procrastination is equally important. It's natural to experience setbacks and moments of procrastination, but instead of berating ourselves, we can use these instances as opportunities for growth and learning.

By acknowledging our mistakes, adjusting our habits as needed, and moving forward with renewed determination, we can break free from the cycle of procrastination and make meaningful progress towards our goals.

By incorporating these strategies into our daily routines and mindset, we can cultivate a productive lifestyle that fosters focus, motivation, and self-improvement. Overcoming procrastination is a gradual process that requires patience and commitment, but by implementing these tips and techniques consistently, we can transform our productivity levels and achieve greater success in both our personal and professional endeavours.

Chapter 7: Embracing Change and Adaptability

In today's fast-paced world, change is an ever-present force that shapes our lives in multifaceted ways. The ability to embrace change and be adaptable is not just a valuable skill but a necessary attribute for navigating the complexities of our modern society. As we face an increasingly interconnected and dynamic world, the capacity to respond to change with agility and resilience becomes paramount.

Embracing change entails more than just a superficial acceptance of the new; it requires a profound shift in mindset and perspective. It involves letting go of rigid expectations and embracing uncertainty with a sense of curiosity and openness. This mindset shift allows us to view change not as a threat but as an opportunity for growth and self-discovery. By remaining flexible and adaptable, we can navigate the ebb and flow of life's transitions with grace and composure.

A growth mindset serves as the foundation for embracing change effectively. This mindset is characterized by a belief in one's ability to learn and grow, even in the face of challenges and setbacks. Individuals with a growth mindset see change as a chance to expand their horizons, build new skills, and develop resilience in the face of adversity. By cultivating a growth mindset, we can approach change with a sense of optimism and a willingness to step outside our comfort zones.

Adaptability, as a core aspect of embracing change, involves a willingness to pivot and adjust to new circumstances. It requires a certain level of flexibility and openness to new ideas and experiences. Being adaptable means not only responding to change but actively seeking out opportunities for growth and innovation.

It involves a continuous process of learning and unlearning, as we adapt to the evolving demands of our environment. Emotional intelligence plays a crucial role in how we navigate change and uncertainty. By cultivating self-awareness, empathy, and effective communication skills, we can navigate the complexities of human emotions and relationships with sensitivity and compassion.

Emotional intelligence allows us to manage our own responses to change and understand the perspectives and emotions of others, fostering collaboration and cooperation in times of transition.

In conclusion, embracing change and adaptability is a multifaceted journey that requires a holistic approach to personal growth and development. By fostering a growth mindset, emotional intelligence, and a willingness to learn and evolve, we can navigate change with resilience and grace, embracing the challenges and opportunities that come our way with a sense of purpose and determination.

The Role of Adaptability in Entrepreneurial Success

Adaptability is a fundamental quality that sets successful entrepreneurs apart in the modern business world. In today's rapidly evolving marketplace, the ability to adjust, pivot, and innovate is crucial for staying relevant and competitive. Entrepreneurs who demonstrate a high degree of adaptability are quick to embrace change and are open to exploring new ideas and approaches.

One key aspect of adaptability is flexibility in thinking and decision-making. Adaptable entrepreneurs are not bound by convention or tradition; instead, they are willing to challenge the status quo and consider unconventional solutions to problems. This flexibility allows them to respond effectively to shifting market dynamics, emerging technologies, and changing consumer preferences.

Resilience is another important characteristic of adaptable entrepreneurs. They understand that setbacks and failures are a normal part of the entrepreneurial journey and view them as learning opportunities rather than insurmountable obstacles. By maintaining a positive outlook and a growth mindset, adaptable entrepreneurs can bounce back from adversity stronger and more determined than before.

Proactivity is also essential for entrepreneurs looking to cultivate adaptability. By staying informed about industry trends, market developments, and competitive landscape, adaptable entrepreneurs can anticipate changes and adjust their strategies accordingly. They seek feedback from customers, employees, and other stakeholders to identify areas for improvement and innovation, ensuring that they stay ahead of the curve.

Furthermore, adaptable entrepreneurs understand the importance of building a diverse and resilient team. By surrounding themselves with individuals who bring different perspectives, skills, and experiences to the table, entrepreneurs can foster a culture of creativity, collaboration, and continuous improvement. This diversity enables them to adapt more effectively to changing circumstances and capitalize on new opportunities as they arise.

In conclusion, adaptability is a critical trait for entrepreneurs seeking success in today's fast-paced and unpredictable business environment. By cultivating flexibility, resilience, proactivity, and a diverse team, entrepreneurs can position themselves to thrive in the face of uncertainty and emerge stronger and more competitive than ever before. Adaptability is not just a skill—it is a mindset that can drive innovation, growth, and success in the ever-changing landscape of entrepreneurship.

Strategies for Embracing Change in Your Business

Change is a fundamental aspect of business growth and evolution, requiring organizations to constantly adapt to new circumstances and trends to remain competitive in today's fast-paced world. Embracing change is not just about surviving; it is about actively seeking opportunities for growth and innovation.

To foster a culture that embraces change, leaders must cultivate a growth mindset within their teams. Encouraging employees to view change as an opportunity for learning and development can shift their perspective from one of resistance to one of curiosity and potential. This mindset shift can pave the way for creativity and new ideas to flourish within the organization.

Open and transparent communication is essential when navigating through periods of change. Keeping employees informed about the reasons behind impending changes and the intended outcomes can help alleviate anxieties and uncertainties.

It is crucial to provide a platform for dialogue where employees feel comfortable expressing their concerns, ideas, and feedback. By involving employees in the change process, leaders can harness their insights and perspectives to drive successful implementation.

Supporting employees through change involves more than just communicating the what and why; it also requires providing the necessary training and resources to help them adapt effectively. Investing in professional development opportunities and coaching can empower employees to acquire new skills and competencies, enabling them to thrive in the evolving business landscape.

Flexibility is key when navigating through change. Business environments are constantly shifting, and leaders must remain agile and adaptable to respond to emerging challenges and opportunities. Being open to new ideas, feedback, and approaches can help organizations stay ahead of the curve and capitalize on transformative moments.

Monitoring progress is essential during times of change. Regularly assessing the impact of implemented changes allows leaders to identify what is working well and where adjustments may be needed. By remaining vigilant and proactive in evaluating outcomes, leaders can make informed decisions to steer the organization in the right direction.

Celebrating successes along the change journey is vital for maintaining morale and momentum. Recognizing and rewarding the hard work and achievements of employees can motivate them to continue embracing change and driving innovation within the organization.

In conclusion, embracing change is not just a necessity; it is an opportunity for growth and transformation. By fostering a culture that values adaptability, communication, collaboration, continual learning, and resilience, organizations can thrive amidst uncertainty and emerge stronger than ever before.

Cultivating a Mindset of Flexibility and Innovation

In today's dynamic and unpredictable world, the ability to remain flexible and innovative is more crucial than ever before. As we navigate through the complexities of modern life, cultivating a mindset that embraces change, welcomes challenges, and seeks out new opportunities can be the difference between thriving and merely surviving.

Flexibility is a key characteristic that allows individuals and organizations to adapt to shifting circumstances, pivot strategies when needed, and respond effectively to unforeseen events. It involves the willingness to embrace uncertainty, let go of rigid structures, and approach situations with an open mind. Embracing flexibility can lead to increased resilience, improved decision-making abilities, and enhanced problem-solving skills.

Innovation, on the other hand, is the engine that drives progress and propels us forward into uncharted territories. It involves thinking creatively, challenging conventional wisdom, and actively seeking out novel solutions to existing problems. Innovation thrives in environments where risk-taking is encouraged, failure is seen as a stepping stone to success, and experimentation is valued as a means of discovery.

Mindset Mastery for Entrepreneurs: Unlocking Your Full Potential

To truly foster a culture of flexibility and innovation, it is important to nurture a growth mindset. This mindset is rooted in the belief that our abilities are not fixed traits but can be developed and improved over time through effort and practice. By adopting a growth mindset, individuals are more likely to view challenges as opportunities for growth, setbacks as learning experiences, and feedback as a valuable tool for improvement.

Curiosity and openness to new experiences are also essential components of a flexible and innovative mindset. By maintaining a sense of curiosity about the world around us, seeking out diverse perspectives, and actively engaging with new ideas, we can expand our knowledge, challenge our assumptions, and spark creativity. Being open to new possibilities allows us to break free from traditional thinking patterns, explore uncharted territories, and uncover innovative solutions to complex problems.

Building a strong support network of mentors, collaborators, and allies can further enhance our ability to be flexible and innovative. Surrounding ourselves with individuals who challenge, inspire, and support us can provide valuable insights, diverse perspectives, and access to resources that can fuel our creativity and drive innovation. Collaboration and teamwork not only foster a sense of belonging and community but also enable us to combine our strengths and talents to tackle complex challenges and generate groundbreaking ideas.

Emotional intelligence plays a critical role in supporting our flexibility and innovation efforts. By developing our ability to recognize and manage our own emotions, empathize with others, and navigate interpersonal dynamics effectively, we can build strong relationships, resolve conflicts constructively, and create a positive work environment that fosters creativity and innovation. Emotional intelligence allows us to communicate effectively, build trust, and inspire others to join us in our quest for innovation and growth.

Moreover, embracing a culture of continuous learning and improvement is essential for sustaining flexibility and innovation over the long term. By staying abreast of emerging trends, seeking out opportunities for growth and development, and actively expanding our knowledge and skills, we can remain competitive in today's rapidly evolving landscape.

A commitment to lifelong learning not only keeps us agile and adaptable but also empowers us to stay ahead of the curve and drive innovation in our personal and professional endeavours.

In conclusion, the ability to be flexible and innovative is a fundamental skill set that can empower individuals to thrive in the face of uncertainty, adapt to change, and unlock their full potential.

By cultivating a growth mindset, fostering curiosity, building a strong support network, honing emotional intelligence, and embracing a culture of continuous learning, we can create a foundation for success that enables us to navigate challenges, seize opportunities, and make a lasting impact in a world that is constantly changing.

Chapter 8: Maintaining Motivation and Resilience

In the labyrinthine pursuit of our dreams, the essence of maintaining motivation and resilience transcends mere persistence; it embodies an unwavering dedication to our deepest aspirations. As we traverse the shifting landscapes of ambition, the union of a clear sense of purpose and an indomitable spirit emerges as the foundation upon which we build our path to greatness.

At the core of sustaining motivation lies the profound understanding of one's intrinsic why – the pulsating heartbeat that propels us forward even in the darkest of times. When we attune ourselves to this inner resonance, we tap into an infinite wellspring of motivation that transcends fleeting obstacles. Continuously anchoring our goals to our core values and passions imbues our journey with meaning and power, fuelling our spirit with a relentless vitality that defies all odds.

Resilience, the silent sentinel of our ambitions, beckons us to embrace challenges as crucibles for growth and transformation. Rather than viewing setbacks as barriers, we are called to see them as gateways to mastery and self-discovery. Nurturing a resilient mindset allows us to bend without breaking, to adapt without compromising our essence, and to emerge from adversity as refined steel – stronger, wiser, and more resilient than before.

The practice of self-care emerges as a sacred ritual in the sanctum of motivation and resilience, nourishing our beings with a balm of gentle compassion and unwavering support. Prioritizing our physical, emotional, and mental well-being becomes a cornerstone upon which we fortify our inner citadel against the ravages of doubt and despair.

Cultivating a repertoire of soul-nourishing activities, alongside forging bonds with kindred spirits who lift us higher in times of need, anchors us to a sanctuary of strength and solace amidst life's tempestuous seas.

Adversity, the great alchemist of our destinies, unveils its hidden treasures to those who dare to walk its crucible with courage and grace. By transmuting setbacks into opportunities for growth, by kindling a fierce belief in our capabilities, and by surrendering to the sacred dance of challenge and transformation, we ascend to the echelons of our highest selves.

In the tapestry of motivation and resilience, we discover not just the power to endure but the grace to transcend, forging a legacy of unwavering determination and indomitable spirit that echoes through the annals of time.

Finding Your Purpose and Passion in Entrepreneurship

As an aspiring entrepreneur, finding your purpose and passion in entrepreneurship is a multifaceted and introspective journey that delves into the very core of who you are and what you wish to achieve. It requires a deep understanding of your values, beliefs, and motivations, as well as a clear vision of the impact you aspire to make in the world.

Understanding your values and beliefs is the foundation upon which your entrepreneurial journey is built. Take the time to reflect on what matters most to you, what principles you hold dear, and what kind of legacy you wish to leave behind. Your values will serve as your compass, guiding you in making decisions that are in alignment with your true self and helping you navigate the complexities of entrepreneurship with integrity and authenticity.

Passion, often referred to as the driving force behind success, is another essential element in finding purpose in entrepreneurship. It is the intense desire and enthusiasm that propels you forward, fuels your creativity, and sustains you through the inevitable challenges that arise along the way.

Identifying your passion involves uncovering what truly excites and energizes you, what brings you joy and fulfilment in the work that you do. Exploring different industries, niches, and business opportunities can be a valuable exercise in uncovering where your true passion lies. Consider your past experiences, skills, and interests, and pay attention to activities that light a fire within you.

Your passion is not just a fleeting interest but a profound sense of purpose that fuels your entrepreneurial endeavours and attracts like-minded individuals who share your enthusiasm and vision. Integrating your purpose and passion into your business strategy is essential for building a sustainable and meaningful venture.

Your purpose serves as the north star that guides your business decisions, ensuring that every action you take is aligned with your higher mission and values. Your passion infuses your work with energy and dedication, inspiring others to join you on your entrepreneurial journey and contributing to a positive impact in the world.

By embracing your purpose and passion in entrepreneurship, you not only create a successful business but also pave the way for a more fulfilling and purpose-driven life. Stay true to your beliefs, follow your heart, and let your values and passion guide you towards building a business that not only brings financial success but also leaves a lasting impact on the lives of others.

Techniques for Staying Motivated During Tough Times

In times of challenges and obstacles, it can be difficult to stay motivated and focused on our goals. However, these tough times are when our resilience and determination are truly tested. Here are some techniques to help you stay motivated during tough times:

1. Remember Your Why: Reconnect with the reasons why you started on this journey in the first place. Remind yourself of your goals, dreams, and aspirations, and visualize the end result to reignite your passion and motivation. Understanding the underlying purpose behind your efforts can provide a powerful driving force to keep you moving forward when faced with adversity.

2. Break It Down: When faced with overwhelming situations, break down your goals into smaller, manageable tasks. By breaking your objectives into bite-sized pieces, you can focus on one step at a time, making the process more manageable and less daunting. This approach not only helps you stay organized but also allows you to track your progress and celebrate each small victory as you move closer to your ultimate goal.

3. Seek Support: Surrounding yourself with a supportive network of friends, family, or mentors can significantly impact your ability to stay motivated during tough times. Having a solid support system provides encouragement, guidance, and a sense of community that can help you overcome challenges and stay focused on your path. It's important to lean on these individuals for advice, motivation, or simply a listening ear when you need it most.

4. Practice Self-Compassion: Treat yourself with kindness and understanding, especially when facing setbacks or failures. Acknowledge that tough times are a natural part of any journey and that making mistakes is an essential aspect of growth and learning. By practicing self-compassion, you can cultivate resilience and bounce back from challenges with renewed strength and determination.

5. Stay Positive: Maintaining a positive attitude and mindset is key to navigating tough times with grace and resilience. Even when faced with adversity, focus on finding the silver linings in every situation and cultivate a sense of gratitude for the lessons learned along the way. Positivity can be a powerful tool in helping you overcome obstacles and stay motivated, no matter how difficult the circumstances may seem.

6. Take Breaks and Rest: Listening to your body and mind is crucial during challenging periods. It's essential to prioritize self-care and allow yourself moments of rest and relaxation to recharge and rejuvenate. Taking breaks can prevent burnout, restore your energy levels, and help you maintain the motivation needed to persevere through tough times.

7. Find Inspiration: Surround yourself with sources of inspiration that uplift and motivate you. Whether it's through reading inspiring books, listening to motivational podcasts, watching TED talks, or connecting with like-minded individuals, seek out sources of inspiration that resonate with your goals and values. Drawing energy from these sources can reinvigorate your motivation and provide you with the drive to push through challenges and obstacles with renewed vigour.

8. Cultivate Mindfulness: Practicing mindfulness can help you stay grounded and present, even in the midst of difficult circumstances. By focusing on the present moment and acknowledging your thoughts and emotions without judgment, you can cultivate a sense of inner peace and resilience that enables you to navigate tough times with clarity and composure. Mindfulness practices such as meditation, deep breathing exercises, or simply taking a moment to pause and center yourself can be powerful tools in maintaining your motivation and focus during challenging periods.

9. Set Realistic Expectations: It's important to set realistic expectations for yourself during tough times. Recognize that progress may be slower than anticipated, setbacks may occur, and obstacles may arise along the way. By managing your expectations and being flexible in your approach, you can adapt to changing circumstances and stay motivated to continue moving forward, even when faced with challenges.

10. Reflect and Learn: Use tough times as opportunities for reflection and growth. When faced with obstacles or setbacks, take the time to evaluate what went wrong, what lessons you can learn from the experience, and how you can adjust your approach moving forward. By viewing challenges as learning opportunities and embracing the mindset of continuous improvement, you can cultivate resilience, adaptability, and a strong sense of motivation that propels you forward through even the toughest of times.

By incorporating these strategies into your mindset and daily practices, you can cultivate a deep sense of motivation that empowers you to persevere through challenges and obstacles, emerging stronger and more resilient on the other side. Remember that tough times are temporary and that your ability to stay motivated and focused will ultimately lead you to success and fulfilment in the long run.

Building Resilience to Bounce Back from Setbacks

In the journey of life, setbacks are inevitable companions that test our resilience and fortitude. How we adapt and respond to these challenges can define our character and shape our future. Building resilience is like forging a strong armor that can withstand the blows of adversity and emerge even stronger on the other side.

Resilience is not just about bouncing back from setbacks; it's about growing through adversity and finding the inner strength to face life's ups and downs with courage and grace. It involves cultivating a mindset that is both optimistic and realistic, acknowledging the hardships while holding onto hope for a brighter tomorrow.

One key aspect of building resilience is developing self-awareness. Understanding our own strengths, weaknesses, and triggers can help us navigate setbacks more effectively and bounce back quicker. By knowing ourselves deeply, we can identify our coping mechanisms, leverage our strengths, and seek support when needed.

It's also essential to cultivate a positive mindset that sees setbacks as opportunities for growth and learning. Embracing a growth mindset allows us to view failures as stepping stones towards success, not as roadblocks. Practicing gratitude and focusing on the things we can control can help shift our perspective during challenging times.

Building a strong support system is another crucial component of resilience. Surrounding ourselves with people who uplift and support us, who can provide encouragement and advice when we're facing challenges, can make a significant difference in how we navigate setbacks. Connecting with others and seeking help when needed can bolster our resilience and help us weather the storms of life.

Self-care is a vital aspect of resilience. Taking care of our physical, emotional, and mental well-being allows us to recharge and refuel our internal resources. Engaging in activities that bring us joy and relaxation, practicing mindfulness and self-compassion, and prioritizing rest and rejuvenation are all essential elements of self-care that can help us build resilience in the face of adversity.

In conclusion, building resilience is a lifelong journey that requires practice, perseverance, and self-reflection. By cultivating a positive mindset, developing self-awareness, building a support system, practicing self-care, and embracing failure as a learning opportunity, we can strengthen our resilience and face setbacks with resilience and determination.

Remember, setbacks are not the end of the road but opportunities for growth and transformation. With resilience as our ally, we can navigate life's challenges with courage and resilience, emerging stronger and more resilient than before.

Chapter 9: Empowering Your Mindset for Success

Achieving success is a multifaceted journey that requires more than just surface-level efforts. To truly empower your mindset for success, it is essential to delve deeper into your inner workings and address underlying beliefs, habits, and patterns that may be influencing your approach to achieving your goals.

Self-awareness plays a crucial role in empowering your mindset for success. Take the time to reflect on your values, motivations, and fears. Understanding what drives you and what holds you back can help you make informed decisions and align your actions with your aspirations. Journaling, meditation, or seeking guidance from a therapist or coach can aid in enhancing your self-awareness and uncovering subconscious barriers that may be impeding your progress.

Furthermore, cultivating emotional intelligence is paramount in empowering your mindset for success. Emotional intelligence encompasses the ability to recognize and manage your emotions effectively, as well as understand and empathize with others' feelings. By developing emotional intelligence, you can navigate interpersonal relationships, handle stress and pressure, and make sound decisions based on a blend of logic and intuition.

Practicing mindfulness, engaging in self-reflection, and seeking feedback from trusted individuals can aid in enhancing your emotional intelligence and strengthening your interpersonal skills. Additionally, adopting a lifelong learning mindset is integral to empowering your mindset for success. Embrace curiosity, continuous growth, and a willingness to adapt to new information and ideas. Stay humble and seek opportunities for personal and professional development to expand your knowledge base and skill set.

Mindset Mastery for Entrepreneurs: Unlocking Your Full Potential

Embrace failure as a learning opportunity rather than a setback, viewing mistakes as stepping stones toward improvement and innovation. By maintaining a growth-oriented mindset, you can fuel your creativity, resilience, and adaptability in the pursuit of success.

Moreover, prioritizing self-care and well-being is crucial in empowering your mindset for success. Nurture your physical health, mental well-being, and emotional resilience to sustain your energy and focus in the face of challenges. Develop a self-care routine that incorporates exercise, healthy nutrition, adequate rest, and mindfulness practices to recharge your body and mind.

Cultivate a supportive environment that fosters your well-being, surrounds yourself with positive influences, and sets boundaries to protect your energy and mental health. In essence, empowering your mindset for success transcends surface-level strategies and requires a holistic approach that addresses self-awareness, emotional intelligence, continuous learning, and well-being.

By delving deeper into your inner landscape and incorporating these principles into your daily life, you can elevate your mindset, enhance your performance, and unlock your full potential on the path to success.

The Mindset Habits of Successful Entrepreneurs

Successful entrepreneurs possess a unique mindset that sets them apart from the rest. It's not just about having a good idea or a solid business plan—it's about how they approach challenges, setbacks, and opportunities on a daily basis. In this extended version of the chapter, we will explore in even greater depth the mindset habits that contribute to the success of these driven individuals.

One crucial mindset habit that successful entrepreneurs embody is adaptability. They understand that the business landscape is constantly evolving, and they must be willing to pivot, adjust, and innovate to stay ahead. This flexibility allows them to navigate changing market conditions, customer preferences, and technological advancements with ease.

By embracing change and being open to new ways of doing things, they can capitalize on emerging trends and stay relevant in a fast-paced world. Moreover, successful entrepreneurs are masters of resilience. They recognize that failure is not the end but rather a stepping stone to success. When faced with setbacks, they bounce back quickly, learn from their mistakes, and use those lessons to fuel their next endeavour.

Mindset Mastery for Entrepreneurs: Unlocking Your Full Potential

This resilience allows them to weather the inevitable ups and downs of entrepreneurship and emerge stronger and more determined than before. In addition to adaptability and resilience, successful entrepreneurs also prioritize continuous learning and personal development. They invest time and resources into expanding their knowledge and honing their skills, whether through formal education, mentorship, networking, or self-study.

By staying curious and committed to growth, they ensure they are always at the forefront of industry trends and best practices. Furthermore, successful entrepreneurs understand the power of collaboration and teamwork. They surround themselves with talented individuals who complement their own strengths and skills, forming a cohesive team that can tackle challenges together.

By fostering a culture of trust, communication, and mutual respect, they create an environment where everyone can thrive and contribute to the company's success. Successful entrepreneurs also possess a strong sense of vision and purpose. They have a clear understanding of what they want to achieve and why they are pursuing their entrepreneurial endeavours. This clarity of purpose not only guides their decision-making and goal-setting but also motivates them to persevere through obstacles and setbacks.

By staying focused on their long-term objectives, they can maintain momentum and drive towards success. Moreover, successful entrepreneurs are adept at managing risk and uncertainty. They understand that entrepreneurship inherently involves taking calculated risks and facing unknown outcomes.

By carefully weighing the potential rewards against the potential downsides, they make informed decisions that mitigate risk while maximizing potential rewards. This ability to navigate ambiguity and make tough choices sets them apart as savvy and strategic business leaders.

In conclusion, the mindset habits of successful entrepreneurs go beyond just having a good business idea—they are rooted in adaptability, resilience, continuous learning, collaboration, vision, purpose, risk management, and a relentless drive for growth and improvement.

By cultivating and embodying these mindset habits in your own entrepreneurial journey, you can position yourself for success and make a lasting impact in the world of business.

Implementing Mindset Mastery Techniques in Your Daily Life

Mastering your mindset is a lifelong journey that requires continual dedication and practice to cultivate a resilient and growth-oriented approach to life. By incorporating a comprehensive set of mindset mastery techniques into your daily routines, you can unlock your full potential and achieve sustainable success in all areas of your life.

1. Morning Routine: Your morning routine sets the tone for the entire day, shaping your mindset and influencing your actions. Begin each day with positive affirmations that resonate with your goals and values. Visualize yourself achieving your aspirations with clarity and confidence, embedding a sense of motivation and purpose within you. Meditation can also play a vital role in centering your mind, enhancing focus, and promoting a state of inner calm essential for navigating the day's challenges with a clear perspective.

2. Gratitude Practice: Gratitude is a potent force that cultivates a profound shift in perspective, guiding your focus towards abundance and appreciation for the blessings present in your life. Keeping a gratitude journal allows you to reflect on the moments of joy, kindness, and growth that you experience daily. Expressing gratitude not only promotes a positive mindset but also fosters deeper connections with others and engenders a sense of interconnectedness and harmony within your life.

3. Challenge Negative Thoughts: Our minds are complex and often prone to negativity bias, leading us to harbour self-limiting beliefs and doubts that hinder our growth. When negative thoughts surface, practice cognitive reframing by questioning their accuracy and validity. Transform these thoughts into empowering and constructive statements that redirect your focus towards solutions and opportunities. Embracing a mindset of possibility and resilience enables you to overcome obstacles with grace and determination, fostering breakthroughs and personal transformation.

4. Goal Setting: Setting clear and achievable goals serves as a compass, guiding your actions and decisions towards tangible outcomes. Break down your larger goals into smaller, actionable steps, creating a roadmap that outlines your progress and milestones. Celebrate each achievement, no matter how small, reinforcing a positive mindset rooted in self-belief and progress. Remain adaptable and flexible in your approach, adjusting your strategies as needed to navigate challenges and stay aligned with your overarching vision.

5. Surround Yourself with Positivity: The environment we immerse ourselves in and the company we keep significantly influence our mindset and emotional well-being. Surround yourself with individuals who support and uplift you, fostering a community of positivity and inspiration. Limit exposure to negative influences, whether through social media curations, mindful news consumption, or setting boundaries with toxic relationships. Cultivating a supportive ecosystem empowers you to maintain a resilient and optimistic mindset amidst life's inevitable ups and downs.

6. Practice Self-Care: Self-care is a profound act of self-love and nourishment that sustains your overall well-being and mindset resilience. Prioritize activities that nurture your physical, mental, and emotional health, such as regular exercise, nutritious eating habits, quality sleep, and stress-relieving practices like mindfulness and relaxation techniques. Investing in your self-care empowers you to show up as your best self, equipped with the energy and vitality needed to navigate life's challenges and seize opportunities with confidence and grace.

7. Reflect and Learn: Reflection serves as a powerful tool for self-awareness and personal growth, allowing you to glean insights from your experiences and evolve continually. Embrace both successes and setbacks as valuable learning opportunities, reframing failures as stepping stones towards growth and resilience. Adopting a growth mindset that views challenges as catalysts for development equips you with the resilience and curiosity needed to embrace change, learn from adversity, and evolve into the best version of yourself.

Mindset Mastery for Entrepreneurs: Unlocking Your Full Potential

By immersing yourself in these mindset mastery techniques and integrating them seamlessly into your daily routines, you embark on a transformative journey of self-discovery and personal growth.

Embrace the power of consistency, dedication, and a steadfast commitment to your mindset evolution to unlock the boundless potential within you and create a life brimming with fulfilment, purpose, and success.

Celebrating Your Wins and Reflecting on Your Growth

Let's talk about the profound practice of celebrating wins and reflecting on personal growth, highlighting the importance of these actions in fostering a positive mindset and personal development.

Celebrating your wins, no matter how big or small, is a crucial part of maintaining motivation and self-confidence. By taking the time to acknowledge and honour your achievements, you are reinforcing a sense of accomplishment and building momentum for future endeavours. Celebrating wins can be as simple as treating yourself to a small reward, sharing your success with others, or taking a moment to reflect on the hard work and effort that went into reaching your goal.

Reflection on personal growth involves looking back on your journey and recognizing the progress and development you have experienced. It allows you to see how far you have come, the obstacles you have overcome, and the skills you have gained along the way. Reflecting on your growth not only provides a sense of pride and satisfaction but also offers valuable insights into your strengths, weaknesses, and areas for improvement.

Moreover, celebrating wins and reflecting on personal growth are essential tools for maintaining a positive mindset and nurturing self-awareness. By actively engaging in these practices, you can cultivate a sense of gratitude, resilience, and motivation that will empower you to continue striving for success in all areas of your life.

In conclusion, taking the time to celebrate your wins and reflect on your personal growth is a powerful practice that can enhance your overall well-being and foster a sense of fulfilment and purpose.

Embrace these practices wholeheartedly, and watch as they propel you further along the path to your dreams and aspirations. Furthermore, celebrating wins not only boosts your confidence but also reinforces positive behaviours and habits, as you are acknowledging the efforts you put into achieving your goals.

This positive reinforcement can lead to increased motivation, productivity, and a greater sense of self-belief. On the other hand, reflecting on personal growth allows you to learn from past experiences, both successes, and failures, and use that knowledge to continue improving and evolving.

It enables you to identify areas where you excel and areas where you can focus on growth, ultimately leading to a more well-rounded and self-aware individual. By incorporating these practices into your daily routine, you are actively investing in your personal development and overall well-being.

They serve as reminders of your capabilities and potential, pushing you to strive for continued growth and success in all aspects of your life.

Chapter 10: Sustaining Mindset Mastery for Long-Term Success

In the journey towards sustaining mindset mastery for long-term success, it is essential to delve deeper into the intricacies of maintaining a growth mindset beyond initial development. While developing a growth mindset is foundational, the ability to consistently uphold this positive mindset requires ongoing effort and dedication to reinforce positive beliefs and behaviours.

Consistent practice is the cornerstone of sustaining mindset mastery. Engaging in regular mindset exercises, such as challenging negative thoughts and reframing them in a positive light, setting specific and measurable goals aligned with growth, and taking deliberate actions towards those goals, can significantly enhance mindset resilience.

By continuously working on strengthening neural pathways associated with growth mindset principles, individuals can more effectively navigate setbacks and challenges by drawing on their ingrained positive thinking patterns. Creating a supportive environment plays a pivotal role in the sustainability of mindset mastery.

Surrounding oneself with like-minded individuals who share similar growth-oriented values and beliefs can provide crucial support, encouragement, accountability, and inspiration. These positive influences can help reinforce a growth mindset mindset and offer a sense of community that fosters continued personal and professional development.

Conversely, minimizing exposure to negative influences and toxic relationships that undermine growth mindset can protect and nurture the mindset's strength and resilience. Self-care is a fundamental component of maintaining a growth mindset over the long term. Prioritizing physical health through regular exercise, proper nutrition, and sufficient sleep is essential for overall well-being. Mental well-being can be nurtured through practices such as mindfulness, meditation, journaling, and seeking professional support when needed.

Emotional balance can be cultivated through self-compassion, self-awareness, and effective stress management techniques. By tending to these aspects of self-care, individuals can operate from a place of strength and resilience, better equipped to face challenges and setbacks with a growth-oriented mindset.

Celebrating small wins and achievements is a powerful strategy for reinforcing a growth mindset. Recognizing progress, no matter how incremental, instils a sense of accomplishment and motivation to keep striving for larger goals. Cultivating a habit of gratitude and acknowledging one's efforts and achievements can boost self-confidence and sustain motivation during challenging times.

By cultivating a mindset of gratitude and recognizing the journey's milestones along the way, individuals can stay motivated and resilient in pursuit of their long-term objectives. In essence, sustaining mindset mastery is a multidimensional process that requires a holistic approach encompassing consistent practice, a supportive environment, proactive self-care habits, and the acknowledgment of successes – no matter how small.

By actively engaging in these strategies, individuals can cultivate a resilient growth mindset that serves as a solid foundation for long-term success, fulfilment, and well-being.

Creating a Mindset Maintenance Plan for Continued Growth

As you embark on your journey of personal growth and mindset mastery, it is crucial to create a maintenance plan that will support your continued development. A mindset maintenance plan involves regular check-ins, reflections, and adjustments to ensure that you stay on track and continue to grow.

Start by setting aside dedicated time each week to review your progress, reflect on your mindset, and identify any areas that need improvement. This could be a weekend journaling session or a set time each morning to meditate and visualize your goals.

During these check-ins, ask yourself the following questions:

1. What positive changes have I noticed in my mindset and behaviour since starting this journey?

2. Are there any recurring negative thought patterns or beliefs that are holding me back?

3. What goals have I achieved, and what obstacles have I faced along the way?

4. How have I been practicing self-care and self-compassion to support my mindset growth?

5. What new habits or practices have I implemented that have positively impacted my mindset?

Reflecting on these questions can provide valuable insights into your mindset journey and help you identify areas for improvement. It's important to acknowledge both your successes and your challenges with a sense of compassion and understanding.

In addition to self-reflection, consider seeking support from a mentor, coach, or community of like-minded individuals who can provide guidance, accountability, and encouragement on your mindset mastery path. Surrounding yourself with positive influences and resources can help accelerate your growth and provide new perspectives on your journey.

Remember that mindset mastery is not a destination but a continuous process of growth and evolution. Embrace the journey, stay committed to your development, and be open to learning from every experience along the way. With dedication and persistence, you will cultivate a resilient and empowered mindset that propels you towards your goals and dreams.

As you deepen your understanding of mindset maintenance, consider incorporating mindfulness practices, such as meditation, deep breathing exercises, or gratitude journaling, into your routine. These practices can help you cultivate self-awareness, reduce stress, and improve your overall well-being.

Furthermore, explore the power of affirmations and visualization techniques to reinforce positive beliefs and goals in your mind. By regularly affirming your capabilities and visualizing your desired outcomes, you can reprogram your subconscious mind for success and abundance.

Additionally, prioritize self-care activities that nourish your body, mind, and soul, such as exercise, healthy eating, adequate rest, and engaging in activities that bring you joy. Taking care of yourself holistically will fuel your mindset growth and provide you with the energy and resilience needed to overcome challenges.

Ultimately, mindset maintenance is a holistic practice that requires consistency, self-awareness, and a commitment to personal growth. By integrating these strategies into your routine and staying dedicated to your mindset mastery journey, you will continue to evolve and thrive in every aspect of your life.

Seeking Ongoing Support and Education for Mindset Development

As an entrepreneur, you should understand the profound impact that mindset development has on your creative output and overall success. The journey towards mastering your mindset is a continuous process that requires dedication, reflection, and a growth-oriented mindset. While your accomplishments may already attest to your resilience and determination, embracing the ongoing nature of mindset growth can unlock new levels of creativity, resilience, and fulfilment in your writing career and personal life.

Surrounding yourself with a diverse and supportive community can be a catalyst for your mindset development. By engaging in deep conversations, sharing experiences, and exchanging ideas with individuals who challenge and inspire you, you create a rich tapestry of perspectives that can fuel your creative process and expand your worldview. This sense of belonging and connection not only fosters a sense of community but also provides a platform for mutual growth and collaboration.

Mindset Mastery for Entrepreneurs: Unlocking Your Full Potential

In addition to external support, cultivating a practice of self-reflection and introspection is essential for deepening your mindset. Taking time to explore your beliefs, values, and thought patterns can unearth unconscious biases, limiting beliefs, and self-imposed barriers that may be hindering your growth. Journaling, meditation, or therapy can be powerful tools for uncovering these hidden aspects of your mindset and catalysing profound transformation.

Furthermore, investing in your ongoing education and personal development is a cornerstone of deepening your mindset mastery. By immersing yourself in a diverse range of learning experiences, from studying psychology and philosophy to exploring different artistic mediums and disciplines, you expand your cognitive flexibility and creative potential. This commitment to lifelong learning not only enriches your writing practice but also nurtures a growth mindset that thrives on curiosity, adaptability, and continuous improvement.

Seeking guidance from mentors or coaches who embody the qualities and values you aspire to cultivate can provide invaluable support on your mindset development journey. A seasoned mentor can offer practical strategies, emotional support, and personalized insights that help you navigate challenges and capitalize on opportunities.

Their guidance can serve as a compass, guiding you towards your writing goals while fostering resilience, self-awareness, and a deep sense of purpose. By embracing the ongoing nature of mindset growth, connecting with a vibrant community, engaging in self-reflection, investing in continuous learning, and seeking guidance from mentors, you deepen your mindset mastery and unlock new dimensions of creativity, resilience, and fulfilment.

This commitment to personal growth not only enhances your career but also enriches your life with a sense of purpose and meaning that transcends success.

Embracing a Lifetime of Learning and Growth as an Entrepreneur

In the realm of entrepreneurship, the pursuit of growth and continuous learning is not just a matter of professional development but a fundamental aspect of a fulfilling and successful entrepreneurial journey. Embracing a mindset of lifelong learning is not only essential for keeping pace with the rapidly evolving business landscape but also for fostering personal resilience, creativity, and adaptability.

Entrepreneurs who approach their journey with a growth mindset understand that challenges are opportunities for growth and view setbacks as valuable learning experiences. By nurturing a mindset that is open to new possibilities and willing to push boundaries, entrepreneurs can cultivate a sense of curiosity and exploration that drives innovation and long-term success.

A key component of embracing lifelong learning as an entrepreneur is the commitment to self-improvement through continuous education and skill development. This can take many forms, including attending industry conferences and workshops, enrolling in online courses, seeking out mentorship from seasoned professionals, and investing in personal development resources such as books and podcasts.

By actively seeking out learning opportunities and expanding their knowledge base, entrepreneurs are better equipped to navigate complexities, solve problems creatively, and adapt to changing market dynamics.

Moreover, entrepreneurs who prioritize lifelong learning are also avid seekers of feedback and insights from a diverse range of sources. By actively seeking feedback from mentors, peers, customers, and other stakeholders, entrepreneurs can gain valuable perspectives, identify blind spots, and uncover opportunities for improvement. This feedback loop is essential for staying connected to the needs and preferences of their target audience and for continuously refining their products and services to meet evolving demands.

In addition to seeking feedback, entrepreneurs who embrace lifelong learning are also skilled collaborators and networkers. By connecting with other entrepreneurs, industry experts, and thought leaders, entrepreneurs can tap into a wealth of knowledge, share experiences, and exchange ideas that can spark innovation and drive growth. Collaboration not only expands their horizons but also opens up new avenues for partnership, mentorship, and collaboration that can propel their businesses forward.

Furthermore, embracing a lifetime of learning as an entrepreneur requires a willingness to adapt and pivot in response to changing circumstances and market trends. This agility is essential for navigating uncertainties, seizing emerging opportunities, and staying ahead of the curve. Entrepreneurs who remain flexible and open-minded are better positioned to pivot their strategies, iterate on their products, and explore new business models that align with shifting consumer preferences and industry trends.

In conclusion, the journey of entrepreneurship is a continual evolution that demands a commitment to lifelong learning, personal growth, and ongoing adaptation. By cultivating a growth mindset, pursuing self-improvement, seeking feedback and collaboration, and remaining agile in the face of change, entrepreneurs can position themselves for sustained success and meaningful impact in the dynamic and competitive world of business.

Some Final Parting Words

As we arrive at the culmination of this exploration into mastering your mindset, it becomes imperative to delve even deeper into the intricacies of fostering a growth mindset. The principles you have internalized by embracing challenges, nurturing resilience, and fostering a positive outlook serve as the bedrock for unlocking your authentic potential and attaining extraordinary heights.

The essence of developing a growth mindset transcends mere confrontation of challenges; it embodies a profound commitment to embracing the iterative process of learning and development that each obstacle presents. By consciously reframing setbacks as gateways to self-realization and advancement, you align with your inner reservoir of strength and perseverance, facilitating unparalleled personal and professional growth.

Peppering your journey with celebrations of incremental victories assumes crucial importance in sustaining motivation and propelling your trajectory towards success. By acknowledging and commemorating even the smallest milestones, you instil a sense of accomplishment and fortify your belief in your inherent abilities. Remember, success is not an eventuality defined solely by outcome but a transformative odyssey that shapes your character and refines your resolve.

Adopting a regimen of self-care stands as a cornerstone of mindset mastery, nurturing your holistic well-being and bolstering your evolution both inwardly and outwardly. Prioritizing moments of solitude, restoration, and mindfulness is paramount for steering the course of sustained triumph and contentment.

Inculcating a supportive ecosystem of like-minded individuals who champion your growth and endorse your potential is equally instrumental. The nurturing influence of these advocates propels you forward, furnishing invaluable feedback, and bestowing a sense of community and affirmation that ignites your spirit and resilience.

Continuing your odyssey towards mastering your mindset, remain vigilant in your allegiance to new prospects and avenues for advancement. Persist in challenging yourself, articulating lofty aspirations, and transcending the confines of your comfort zone. The roadmap to victory may not invariably be strewn with ease, yet it is through these crucibles that you will unearth the depth of your mettle and potential.

In conclusion, I implore you to remain unwavering in your dedication to personal edification and growth. Your mindset is a potent instrument capable of sculpting your reality and shepherding you towards the life you aspire to lead. Embrace the expedition, hone your focus on your aspirations, and never underestimate the profundity of your capabilities.

May your mindset continue its metamorphosis, guiding you towards a tapestry abundant with success, opulence, and fulfilment. Trust in the evolution of your journey, foster unwavering faith in your abilities, and forever hold close the verity that the power to illuminate your reality resides within you.